The *Invisible* Thread

True Stories of Synchronicity

With

Sunny Dawn Johnston & Friends

OptiMysticPress

Printed in the United States of America
General editing: Connie Gorrell
Cover design: Kris Voelker Designs

OptiMystic Press, Inc.
P.O. Box 6, Woodburn, IN 46797
www.optimystic.press

If unable to purchase this book from your local bookseller, you may order directly from online bookstores or via the publisher's website.

ISBN-13: 978-0692690246
ISBN-10: 0692690247

Library of Congress Control Number: 2016903169

An invisible thread connects those who are destined to meet, regardless of time, place or circumstance. The thread may stretch or tangle but it will never break. May you be open to each thread that comes into your life— the golden ones and the coarse ones—and may you weave them into a brilliant and beautiful life. —Chinese Proverb

DEDICATION

This book is dedicated to the brave storytellers that celebrate the thread that connects each of us to one another and to the Sacred...

To those willing to sit with their vulnerabilities yet stand in their truths; those who are willing to fly and to soar freely to places of the heart, both seen and unseen.

CONTENTS

Sunny Dawn Johnston is a gentle, loving and supportive inspirational teacher, author, motivational speaker and psychic medium. She has helped thousands of people across the country find their personal spiritual connection, recognize and 'own' their natural spiritual gifts, and listen to their inner truth.

What makes Sunny unique is her ability to transform her own inspirational life story into practical tools and knowledge. She teaches through her experience and truly does walk her talk. In December 2003, Sunny founded Sunlight Alliance LLC, a spiritual teaching and healing center in Glendale, Arizona. She followed her guidance and created a place where people could go for support, empowerment, direction and most of all unconditional love.

Sunlight Alliance LLC offers classes on a variety of spiritual subjects such as communicating with your angels, reiki, mediumship, intuitive development, death and dying and many more. These are offered at the healing center as well as thru online streaming, so if you don't live in Arizona, you can still connect with Sunny from the comfort of your own home.

Sunny also facilitates healing retreats in Sedona, Arizona as well as throughout the United States and internationally. Sunny has been featured on many local and national television and radio shows. When Sunny is not traveling or teaching, you can find her in the recording studio working on her next CD and writing her next book. She is the author of the bestselling book *Invoking the Archangels: A 9-Step Process to Healing Your Mind, Body and Soul*. Among Sunny's other books are *No Mistakes, Love Never Ends* and *Living Your Purpose*.

Sunny is actively involved in the spiritual community and frequently conducts informational outreach work. Her workshops and seminars are highly attended throughout the country. She also volunteers her time as a psychic investigator for the international organization FIND ME. This is a not-for-profit organization of Psychic, Investigative, and Canine Search & Rescue (SAR) volunteers working together to provide leads to law enforcement and families of missing persons and homicide. Sunny co-authored her first book *Find Me*, and it is available on her website at **www.sunnydawnjohnston.com**

Sunny resides in Glendale, Arizona with her husband, two children and two dogs. In her spare time, you can find her playing with her Spirit and enjoying time with friends and family. You can learn more about Sunny by visiting her website at **www.sunnydawnjohnston.com**.

Connect with Sunny

Email
sunny@sunnydawnjohnston.com

Websites
www.sunnydawnjohnston.com
www.soulfoodwithsunny.com

Blog
www.sunnydawnjohnston.com/blog

Social Media
www.facebook.com/sunnydawnjohnston
Twitter @SunnyDawn444

CHAPTER ONE

The *Invisible* Thread

By Sunny Dawn Johnston

There comes a time in our lives where we make a decision. Sometimes it is a conscious choice and sometimes it stems from an experience that we can no longer deny. Either way, we arrive at a point in our lives where we know or feel that it is time to move forward. We can no longer live life asleep at the wheel. It is time to wake up and take responsibility for our life and everything in it. It is time to take our power back and *really* live. If you have been feeling guided to look deeper into the synchronicities in your own life, this book has come to you at the perfect time.

My life had been in a downward spiral for many years. As a teenager struggling to find my identity, I hid my intuitive gifts, gave my power away and blamed anyone and everyone else for my problems…and I had a long list of problems. As long as I was able to blame others, I could be a victim. Life was painful, but tolerable. Victimhood allowed me to stay in the background—to hide, to lay down, to give up. It allowed me to pretend that I was not worthy. It was a safe and familiar, albeit uncomfortable, place to be.

One night as I sat in the dense energy following a blowout argument with my boyfriend, warm tears streaming down my face as I rocked my one-year-old son to sleep in my arms, I had an intuitive insight. These insights happened regularly for me, but because the insights were typically positive, I was in no place to allow them in. In fact, they often felt like bee stings—sharp little poking reminders of what I did not have in my life, and did not deserve. These insights occurred in many different ways, but this time it came as a flash in my mind's eye. In this particular vision, my son and I were smiling and happy, playing together and truly enjoying life, but someone else was in the picture as well. I could not see him, but I could feel his presence. I knew it was a man—no, *the* man—the one that would be a father to my son and my best friend. For many, this would bring peace and hope, but for me being in the powerless place I occupied, it brought sadness, frustration, and anger.

These insights are what I often refer to as the **Invisible Thread**. We each have an invisible thread—call it energy, connection, insight, Angels, Spirit, God…it is the invisible thread that connects us to the Spirit world. This connection runs to us and through us, always—and in all ways. My problem was that I was not willing to see the insights. I did not want to hear them. Actually, I did the opposite. I would question them as a way of keeping myself disconnected.

Why receive these so-called visons or gifts if they don't in fact help me? If the vision is not actually attainable? If it just makes things worse? These were my questions, and each time they came, I *did* question. I questioned myself, my guidance, even my angels. I would ask for help, and then not listen. I was stuck in a cycle of victimization that I had placed myself in. I would have moments of empowerment, moments of self-love... and then the doubts would float back in like a big, dark cloud. It was as if I could not tolerate the sunshine of life. It was seemingly too hard to accept my light, my connection, *my invisible thread.*

This darkness seemed comfortable in some ways. The smoke-filled shack we lived in made it hard to breathe in anything life-sustaining. The density of the alcoholic environment was a reminder of which I had allowed myself, and my son, to stay trapped. It was dark, dreary and heavy. I was embarrassed, ashamed and guilt-ridden. The darkness took over my mind. It was easy to stay stuck when all I was willing to see was the pain, the lack and the fear. The stories of "not-being-good-enough" and "why-me?" would circle around in my head daily. It was as if I had a permanent song playing internally that was tuned to "shuffle the shit." I felt crazy, and in some ways, I acted that way, too.

In the midst of the pain of this experience, I became keenly aware that I had lost my path. I had lost my power. I had lost my connection to my invisible thread. How did I lose it? Where did it go? Those were questions I asked myself. Maybe you, too, have asked yourself that from time to time. It seems like a silly question because, of course, we know the answer: *It is all right here.* We know that the connection to Spirit never leaves. However, when you are in a place of tremendous pain and loss it is hard to reach for anything different, let alone better. It was that awareness, that I had lost myself, my path, my power, and most importantly, my connection to the Divine within me that catapulted me in a new direction.

I had been waiting for someone else to take responsibility for my life. I had been hoping that my boyfriend could love me enough to quit drinking, to want to work, to be a better dad, and so forth. What I realized in that defining moment was that I had invested all of my energy, time and heart into him. He didn't take it…**I GAVE IT!** And with that, the biggest realization of my life arrived. The one that changed everything. Are you ready?

I had not actually LOST anything. I had GIVEN it away! Oh, my God, I had it wrong the whole time. He was not taking anything from me. He did not need to. I was giving it all away because then it could be someone else's responsibility, not mine. I could have someone else to blame; and in this way, I could make it okay in my mind when I felt disconnected from Spirit as well. The story I had been telling myself was that I was not good enough, and I did not deserve even the support and help of the Angels.

This realization changed my life. I chose to take my power back. I chose to reconnect with that Light within me. I began to welcome that connection—my invisible thread—back into my life with open and deserving arms; and in doing so, I realized it was time to take personal responsibility for my life and my choices. It was shortly after that when I broke up not only with my boyfriend, but with the unhealthy relationship with *myself.* I began a new, loving and kind relationship with myself and connected with my Spirit again. I began to believe in the vision of a

3

brighter, healthier, happier future with my son and that special someone, yet unknown. The synchronicity in my story is that fourteen months later, that exact vision came true. I met my husband and my son's father. Nine months later we were married, and have lived in love for over twenty-two years.

As I write the introduction to this amazing book, I look over the past twenty-five years of my life with compassion and love. From that young teenage mom living in the shack—insecure, disconnected and in deep pain—to the woman I am today, I know there have been many bumps and blessings on the road of life. I have been very fortunate to experience some of the greatest peaks in life that anyone could encounter: unconditional love, fantastic relationships, incredible health, a successful business supporting others, and the list goes on and on. I have also dipped to those lowest of lows, the valleys that we sometimes struggle to survive: suicide, miscarriages, betrayal, and tragic death. I, like you, have been there...and done that.

What is different now is that I am in appreciation of it all. With each and every hardship, it has expanded me into allowing for more blessings. I have gained a strength that only comes by journeying through this life and all it has to offer. With each and every joy-filled moment, I have learned to breathe it in, receive the love, and accept that I am Spirit embodied and deserve the best of life. Most importantly, the invisible thread, the one that I believe has saved my life many times over by guiding and directing me, is no longer invisible. As I have opened up, believed in, allowed, and surrendered to my innate connection with Spirit, it has strengthened what was once invisible. Although not seen to the naked eye, this connection is evident every single day to my open, believing and receiving eyes.

How did this happen? Well, it wasn't overnight. It was a process of asking and allowing, giving and receiving, opening and healing. Maybe you have found yourself in this place, too? You know what you **don't** want to feel, to think, to do—but you may not know clearly what you **do** want. So ask yourself this question: Am I ready to connect to, and receive the guidance from, Spirit? Am I ready to take the action my soul is crying out for? Am I ready to embrace the connection to my invisible thread?

It is already there. You just need to listen, watch, feel and hear it.

Within the pages of this book you will discover messages of empowerment and stories of synchronicities that could not be ignored by the authors. The great thing is that this thread, the one that ties us all together, that guides us along the way, is there for one and all. As you will read in the following pages, some connect with it through a dream, some feel it through amazing relationships and some find the thread through traumatic loss. Often showing up in the most indescribable form this thread that binds us all has no boundaries and no judgment. It is always there. There is nothing and no one exempt for the connectedness of life. It is the tie the binds our hearts and spirits together.

While reading this book, you yourself will gain intuitive insights as you connect with these amazing authors' stories and the synchronicities they experienced in their lives. You will then begin to look back over your life, peeking into the past and seeing your own invisible thread. What a fantastic journey it is to see that it has always been there…even when you were not aware.

Knowing that everything happens for a reason I know that you are meant to read this book—simply because you have been guided to it. This is how Spirit works. *The Invisible Thread* would not be in your hands right now had your spirit not set up this divine appointment. Are you ready to wake up to the synchronicities in your life? Are you willing to make the choice to see more clearly the ways of Spirit? I believe you already have— by picking up this book. Now, all that is left to do is to begin reading!

CONNIE GORRELL

Author, publisher and speaker *Connie Gorrell* is passionate about helping people create their most authentic path in life. Her experience and wisdom resonates with those striving to make the leap to finding success through adversity, whether on a personal or a professional level. Connie speaks candidly to women in all walks of life, encouraging them to tell their stories. She a highly respected coach, consultant and mentor to her constituents on a global level.

Connie is President of OptiMystic Press, Inc. and the founder of the *DreamSTRONG*™ Foundation, a public charity designed to create inspired change for women and girls through empowerment, enrichment and education. "I want those living unfulfilled lives find the tools and inspiration needed to take control of their situation; to prove to *every* woman that she can live a rich and deserving life and exercise her God-given right to strive for her dreams—no matter what." says Connie. "We *must* tell these stories."

ACKNOWLEDGEMENT

My love and appreciation to Sunny Dawn Johnston for relentlessly nudging me out of the comfort of my 'pain zone' where I found a safe place to play and write. Sincere gratitude to my friend and colleague Shanda Trofe for interweaving her golden threads with mine to co-create this book project and so much more. Eternal grace to my sweet husband, Brent, for walking this incredible journey with me, ever present, and having more faith in me than I had in myself.

DEDICATION

This chapter is dedicated to the warrior spirit of my amazing mother Ruby, to my loving husband Brent, and to the Sun that rose in the west.

SPECIAL DEDICATION TO OUR SONS

Rob, Aaron, Mike, Nick. Sleep peacefully, our angels.

Connect with Connie

Email
connie@conniegorrell.com

Websites
www.conniegorrell.com
www.dreamstrong.org
www.optimystic.press

Social Media
www.facebook.com/conniesgorrell
www.facebook.com.optimysticpress
www.facebook.com/dreamstrong.us
Twitter: @ConnieGorrell

CHAPTER TWO

Dream Strong

By Connie Gorrell

There she is again, that wild-eyed woman, tearing another book to shreds in the back yard, crying the ugly cry and mumbling inaudibly. Is she dismembering book number five? Or is it six? I have lost count. Any astounded onlooker would think she has lost all sense of sanity, but I know better. I know her. She is *me*, and I was expected by some to 'lose it.' I lost it, all right—I lost my dreams.

Expectations are funny things. We are expected to react to certain situations in certain acceptable ways, but unique situations arise sometimes that provide no rules or road signs to guide us safely home. We may even go a little crazy in the process. But who are we to judge?

Between the years 1999 and 2008 my husband and I endured the traumatic losses of all four of our sons. My two, and his two. Tragic news repeatedly delivered by an early morning knock on the door, phone calls, even a text message shattered our lives with unexpected news of four deaths. Shock after stunning shock. A lifetime of dreams—shattered. The song The Impossible Dream (also referred to as The Quest from the play, Man From La Mancha, 1972) says it best...I couldn't bear with unbearable sorrow or run where the brave dare not go. To have a dream after so much tragedy? Impossible.

In the wake of the four funerals, even strangers showered us with gifts of well-meaning and hopeful comfort. Some were in the form of sedatives secretly pressed into my hands by elderly women saying, "Take this, honey. It'll make you feel better." I blankly accepted them but did not partake. Close friends delivered self-help books in earnest attempts to

9

show their love and concern because I am certain they were at a loss for words themselves. We received books on grieving the loss of a child, books on the healing process and books on dealing with trauma. Though emotionally exhausted I genuinely attempted to muster enough energy to read them only to find minimal solace or comfort within their covers. But some, let's say, really lit my already frazzled fuse.

The straw that broke the proverbial camel's back and launched me into the back yard for the first of the tirades came from a book on grieving written by two individuals. In its opening chapter, I found a measure of comfort reading the words, "be gentle with yourself; cry when you need to cry." I felt almost vindicated in the form of relief, finally admitting that I did not always have to be the strong one. But like a blast to my broken heart came the second writer's paraphrased stark message: *Whatever tragedy you are facing, it is God's will and you have no right to question...*

To say I was in a fragile state of mind is an understatement. I had news for the writer. When you find yourself on buckled knees in a cemetery in the dark of night, screaming until no sound comes out, clenching the fresh dirt of your only children's graves in your fists, you *bet* you question the existence of, or reasoning behind, everything you had ever known to be true. At least *I* did. But here's the thing: I survived this phase because I believe that the God of my understanding not only approves but *allows* raw human emotion and questioning. I was allowed to go through the stages of suffrage and was gently escorted back home safely. Did I initially question God and the existence thereof? Oh, you bet I did. Did it last? Thankfully, no. But it was a hard fought process—an all-out battle of wills, through a raging storm, blinding tears and mass exodus of support from people we thought would always be there.

Who, What, When—But, *Why*?

When tragedy strikes, a natural human response is to begin asking the universal questions: *Why? Why* me? *Why* this? *Why* now? Never having been normal to begin with, I never asked why. In my mind there were no explanations on God's green earth that would have brought peace at that time; nothing would explain away such deep losses, and arbitrary and empty explanations of philosophy would not cut it. I only wanted my children back. Asking *why* would merely serve to make me angrier. Trust me, the world did not need angry, crazy Aunt Connie running loose in a grocery store wielding a mobile weapon such as a shopping cart or exhibiting other reckless behaviors such as wearing stretch pants in public.

Though *why* was not in my vocabulary, other questions were hauntingly real: How does one survive the vision of viewing their children's faces in death? Will I will see them every time I close my eyes to sleep? Will dreams become night terrors? Life's aspirations seemed to fade away as an echo waning in the distance. So, who am I now? What will I say when someone innocently asks, "How many children do you have?" There were many painful questions but the most looming unanswered, perhaps the scariest of all was: *Will I dream again*? Where is my legacy? My children lie in eternal repose in the countryside. There will be no future generations, no grandchildren for me to spoil rotten. It would be only my husband, Brent, and me, from this day forward.

Brent and I have been asked many times how our marriage survived the rapid fire tragedies when oftentimes that is not the case with much less than what we had experienced. I can only say this: We never played the 'blame game.' When the first of our sons died, we made a sacred and solemn vow to one another—that very day. We vowed that we had lost enough already and to lose each other could never be an option. We never faltered on that vow though we were destined to travel that tragic road three more times.

Do Nothing When Nothing Works

Grieving from one's inner-most soul perpetuates sheer exhaustion. Though I had no formal plan to end my life, in those raw and early days, I welcomed dying in my sleep. Later, I learned that after my youngest son Aaron's funeral (the third of the four), Brent had his guns removed from our home. I realized the frightening situation I had inflicted on my loving—and also grieving—husband. For the sake of that sweet and loving man and the heartbreak I saw in his eyes each time he looked at me, I resolved to stand up and fight like my life depended on it, because I knew it did.

Fighting through the residual guilt of words left unsaid or feelings left unresolved with my sons had almost incapacitated me to the point of no return. But we are promised that God intervenes when asked. I hit my knees and begged for the strength and stamina to fight. I knew I had to do something, but with no energy I merely wanted to do nothing. So, I did what many would do under similar circumstances…I mowed. I hit the deck of the riding lawn mower and set out on a long summer journey, back and forth.

We live in a hundred and twenty-seven-year-old house on two acres surrounded by lush farm land on all sides. The great outdoors has always been my cathedral where I can connect with the Sacred. During the first few agonizing summers I turned lawn-mowing time (my getting-something-done-while-actually-doing-nothing time) into much needed alone time. It was the perfect set-up for reflection and afforded me the chance to sing loudly, and badly, or cry freely without Brent being aware. He openly agonized when I cried, and I could not bear that. So I disguised my tears—and mowed.

One summer afternoon a few years ago, I was mindlessly mowing, back and forth, this direction and that. I was using the roar of the mower's engine to drown the sounds of my sobs that day. I reveled in the sense of release that I could let my emotions fly while embracing the warmth of the sun and my secret talks with God. A car passed very slowly and I looked up through my tears to see an older couple ogling me quite oddly. In my embarrassment and fragile frame of mind, my first instinct was to stand up, shake my fist in the air and holler, "Hey! What are you looking at, Bub?" but I knew to keep my wimpy ass in the seat. Then, it occurred to me what their conversation must have been.

I imagined the scenario like this: The lady passenger turns to the driver and says, "Oh, honey, look at that woman. She's crying, poor dear—she must *really hate to mow*!" Once it dawned on me what she had said, I fell into hysterical laughter which made me push suddenly on the gas pedal causing me to flip backwards off the lawn mower. Talk about awkward! The couple laid a patch getting out of there.

As I lay in the grass, in pain, looking skyward, laughing and crying simultaneously, something happened. It was as if an angelically soft voice

12

whispered, *"Connie, come back. Honor your sons by living—truly living. Love them more in death than you ever dreamed possible in life. They are alive in you forever."*

That was the day I began to realize that I had not been deserted; I was never alone. God's guidance gave me a lifeline—a spark of crystal clarity to face the tasks before me and a light to show the way. I ached to wake from this recurrent nightmare and desperately wanted something good to rise from the ashes, but it would not happen overnight. As the saying goes, it's not how many times you are knocked down that counts—it's how many times you get back up. Four sons, four funerals. I am not defined by these losses, but rather the manner in which I handle them. Hell on earth exists only if you allow yourself to remain there. Who needs that? I made a promise to myself to fight for my life.

Bottoms Up!

There was a period of time when I introduced myself to the bottom of the heap and resolved that there was simply nowhere else to go. The only thing I knew for sure was that I felt isolated and disassociated from all things previously familiar. Bottom, meet Connie. She's new here. Be gentle, okay? Building a new future from the bottom up meant there were choices to be made, possibilities to be created, and lost dreams to be found.

As I had politely passed on the medications so generously prescribed by elderly women, alcohol also played no part in recovery. Sober, agonizing days turn into weeks while birthdays and holidays painfully rolled by. Crying jags came less frequently but the shadow of those tears never strayed very far, even to this day. I paid a high price, though. Through my agony, I allowed my body to become ill. I know, first hand, that grief can kill you from the inside out if you let it. It can affect your body and mind on a chemical and cellular level.

The heartbroken woman ripping books to shreds in her back yard has journeyed far. The chaotic and crazy moments of confusion ended with the clarity needed to push through the pain and find ways of surviving the unthinkable. I also had to fight my way back to better health. My mission became my passion—to share a message of strength that we are truly stronger than we think, and I set out to prove it. I began writing again and making speaking appearances to share my message, offering comfort and resources to those in need. I have stood, oh so dangerously, on the brink, and I have heard the cries of many.

The Impossible Dream

While dealing with sadness and the illness that had consumed my body I learned the importance of self love and self-care. One day, while in the midst of undergoing medical treatment, I surrendered to my fatigue and took an afternoon nap. In a dream-state I clearly heard my oldest son's voice saying, *"Dream STRONG, Mom."* Sitting straight up in bed I vividly recalled a poignant conversation that took place shortly before he died at age twenty-four.

We were discussing our individual hopes and dreams when Rob asked what I wanted to be when I 'grow up.' After quipping, "Yeah, right," my thoughts silently trailed back to when my boys were small. How I wished I had done things differently when I had the chance—how much better our lives might have been had I not lacked the courage to stand in my own painful truth and admit that I had been in dire need of help. As the conversation continued my son asked the ultimate question: "Mom, what do you *really* dream of doing?" He genuinely wanted to know.

I shared with him my secret dream of writing for publication and having a successful business of my own someday. Then, as an afterthought, I added that I wanted to inspire women to fight for their dreams and make a better life for herself and those she loves. He paused, and then he spoke. I will never forget Robbie's solemn words to me that day: *"Whatever it is you're dreaming of doing, Mom, you have to be strong—and go for it."*

And so it is—DreamSTRONG.

Since the early days after my sons' deaths I wanted to do something in their honor but did not know what to do, or how. In the dreamlike visitation my son had reminded me to live my dream. I set about learning how to start a nonprofit foundation to turn my passion into an organized mission.

I was determined to follow that dream no matter what. Amazingly, the DreamSTRONG™ Foundation became an official 501(c)(3) public charity faster than the attorney or the accounts had ever witnessed in their collective careers—eleven days, to be exact. Ironically, it became official on the thirteenth anniversary of Rob's passing.

Today I know it is possible to *DreamSTRONG* and I am asking that you embrace this for yourself, too. As a donor or a recipient, there is great importance in having a coordinated effort to help those struggling behind us. We face tremendous stressors every day of our lives and many times we become overwhelmed. We may end up confused, disillusioned, and ineffective in our life's journey. Some of us become expert actresses, living a double life, insisting that everything is fine and refusing to grab the life vest—even when it's within our reach. That helps no one. Not us, and certainly not those we love that are trying their best to love us back!

There are women living in similar situations as I had been those years ago—struggling on a daily basis to wear a brave face while secretly falling apart. She may not be on public assistance, but she's barely making ends meet, has no nest egg to depend on, and no means of following her dreams. She may experience the emotional gamut, everything from feeling slightly unsettled to full blown chaos and in need of calculated change in her life. There are women living in high risk and dysfunctional situations in dire need of help. To them, dreams are merely visions one has at night while sleeping. That had been me.

The exhaustion of living a double life and keeping up appearances takes its toll physically, emotionally and spiritually, though only subtly at first. I learned that if I was suffering silently and inwardly, so were those around me. Is this you, too? Everyone pays the price—your spouse or significant other to be sure...but more significantly, your children. I believe that creating a world of better situated women results in less stressed mothers who raise happier children who make a better world. Here is the sacred arc that forms the circle of life—and it starts with women. I recognized that I could never go back and change our life's circumstances, but by God, I could be a voice for others going through similar situations. Today, no one can tell me that their dreams are impossible. *No one.*

Falling away from our authentic purpose can make us hesitant to ask for help in achieving our dream. It's daunting. I know what it feels like to be too misdirected to recognize the need for help. When we do not honor our passion in life, we may find ourselves failing miserably in a job we find unfulfilling, or worse, detest. We become wrapped up in living a double life and making it 'work' for us. We wind up overwhelmed and exhausted and don't know how to break the cycle. We lose sight of our dreams and goals. Meanwhile, dreams and aspirations lay on hold in a quiet corner of our distant memory. I am living, breathing proof that your dreams never die. They are as close as the beating of your heart. Nothing— hear me clearly—*nothing* is impossible.

Let us walk this journey together, side by side. The invisible thread binds us together as we follow the path laid out for us—Spirit guided, to be sure! When you allow your life's passion to shine through, then fully admit and commit that it's time to plant the seeds of your dreams.

Don't waste another precious day. I wasted enough for all of us, though now I know I was being schooled. Honor God, yourself and your loved ones like never before.

Face your fears and feel your passion from the inside out—but seek no further than from within, for you will never, *ever,* find it outside you. Live freely and joyously in confidence knowing that you are never alone. Know that you must, in your own way, *DreamSTRONG!*

To learn more about the DreamSTRONG™ Foundation

visit **www.dreamstrong.org**.

SHANDA TROFE

Shanda Trofe, bestselling author, publisher, and writing coach is the Founder of Spiritual Writers Network, an online community of over 3,000 writers and authors, and President and CEO of Transcendent Publishing and Write from the Heart, LLC. Aptly named the *Authorpreneur Mentor* by her colleagues, Shanda aims to educate aspiring authors not only on the business of writing and publishing, but also how to grow an empire based on the core concepts of their published work.

Shanda is experienced in both fiction and non-fiction writing, specializing in both print and digital publishing, and enjoys assisting authors throughout the entire process, from idea to publication. She understands that each writer has individualized needs, and aims to educate authors on the options available so they can choose the writing and publishing path that's right for them. But first, she works diligently with her clients to lead them through the writing process, helping to find their voice and extract the unique message they possess within.

In addition to working with writers and aspiring authors, Shanda is a Certified Mind, Body and Spirit Practitioner, Angel Therapy Practitioner, and Spiritual Life Coach. She believes by incorporating spiritual practices into her business, she can better serve her clients and lead them to success.

ACKNOWLEDGEMENT

I am blessed and thankful to receive unconditional love and support from my husband, Anthony, who always believes in me, while allowing and encouraging me to follow my dreams and honor my journey. My thanks also goes to Connie Gorrell for walking this part of my journey with me and becoming one of my greatest teachers. Finally, I acknowledge with infinite love and gratitude the inspiration of my mentor and teacher, Sunny Dawn Johnston, the tie that binds us all together.

DEDICATION

This chapter is dedicated to my clients and students who make it all possible. Without you, I would just be a woman with a dream, for you are the reason I do what I do, and helping to make your dreams come true is what I live for.

Connect with Shanda

Email: info@shandatrofe.com

Websites
www.shandatrofe.com
www.transcendentpublishing.com
www.spiritualwritersnetwork.com

Social Media
www.facebook.com/shandatrofe
www.twitter.com/shandatrofe

CHAPTER THREE

Woven Dreams

By Shanda Trofe

There are no coincidences on the path when the soul leads the way.

—Kate Spencer

In 2012 I felt a calling. I was being called to Sunny Dawn Johnston's healing retreat in Sedona, Arizona, yet I didn't know why. What I did know was to have enough trust in myself and the universe to follow my inner guidance. Thank God I listened.

In April of 2012 I travelled to Sedona, alone, not knowing what I was going to learn, or even what I was going to heal, for that matter. I'd never met Sunny before, but I had run across her name online due to our mutual love for angels, and that's when I discovered her upcoming annual Healing Retreat. A strong knowing that I needed to attend the retreat overcame me, so there I was, travelling over 2,000 miles on a mission to heal my life and grow spiritually. That was my intention going in. Unbeknownst to me at the time, it would lead to so much more.

During the retreat I experienced considerable growth. As it turns out, I had some issues from my past to heal in order for me to become the best version of myself and evolve spiritually. Feeling inspired, before leaving the retreat I announced that I was working on a book. I received so much support and praise from the women at the retreat that I felt my declaration to the universe must be followed, so upon returning home I completed that short book on the Law of Attraction, a subject that I feel passionate about and principles I incorporate into my life daily.

Shortly thereafter, Sunny announced that she was working on a compilation book project, *Living Your Purpose with Sunny Dawn*

Johnston and Friends, and there was space in the book to write alongside her as a co-author. I knew I wanted a chapter in that book, and somehow I believed publishing my own book would make me a more desirable candidate. That familiar inner knowing that I needed to take action was alive within me, so I researched publishing options for my own book and that's when I discovered digital publishing. My life was forever changed.

Self-publishing that first small eBook on Amazon may or may not have helped me get a space in Sunny's book, but I was in *and* I had a book of my own under my belt. Utilizing some of the spiritual practices I had learned at the retreat, I was on a mission to find my own life purpose at the time and was doing a lot of inner work to find out what that purpose was. That's when the idea came to me for Spiritual Writers Network.

I had a vision of a platform where spiritual writers could come together and share their writing within a like-minded community. The network would offer the writers, healers, teachers, and artists of the world a place to publish their messages for free, with the intention to raise the world's vibration through love and inspiration, one word at a time.

I quickly realized there was a calling for this type of platform, and within just a few months of its launch we had over a thousand registered writers sharing on the network! Naturally, I felt the urge to offer them more. I had to find a way to broaden the stage for these writers so their wonderful messages could be received in an even greater way. Again, while doing my inner spiritual work, the idea for Transcendent Publishing came to me.

I already knew how to publish digitally on Amazon, since I had just completed my first eBook, so learning to format for print publication was next on my list. I thought, what a nice gift it would be to host writing contests for publication on the network and publish the books in multi-author compilations to be available on Amazon and other distribution channels, so that's what I did. I started running quarterly writing contests for publication, and within the first year I had published hundreds of authors in contest books in both print and digital editions. The service was well received; I was making dreams of publication come true, as many of the contestants were first-time authors, and some even went on to publish their own books through Transcendent Publishing; thus, the company was born.

The next year I felt another calling. This time I was being called to attend Sunny's Mind, Body and Spirit Practitioner Certification, otherwise known as MBS. With a desire to explore my spiritual gifts on a deeper level, I once again found myself on a plane flying solo to Arizona, not knowing what I was getting myself into, just that I had a strong desire to learn and grow spiritually. That inner nudge had returned and I knew well enough to listen.

Sunny's MBS certification program proved to be another life-changing experience for me, for it was at MBS where I met Connie Gorrell. We instantly hit it off, and after leaving the MBS and returning to our separate corners of the earth, we decided to collaborate. Together we came up with fantastic plans—it was like our ideas would feed off each other and before we knew it we'd been on the phone for hours, always hanging up with a project in the works and a clear plan of action. It's through one of those phone sessions where the idea for this book was born, and now here we are, connected in one way or another, by an invisible thread that has brought us all together.

Fast forward to 2016 and it's all come full circle. I continued to work with Sunny as my mentor and teacher through various trainings and she now hires me to work on projects with her. Sunny is not only my teacher and respected mentor, but she's also my colleague and friend. Connie is a special contributor to my 8-Week Book Writing Intensive, where together we coach aspiring authors through the book writing process. Having just returned from a writer's retreat I co-hosted with Sunny and Connie in the Florida Keys, I find there is no better time to write this chapter than now.

You see, I had a surreal moment at that retreat. Looking around the room I discovered not only was I now facilitating an event with my esteemed colleagues, Sunny Dawn Johnston and Connie Gorrell, but the room was filled with writers from Spiritual Writers Network, alumni from the Book Writing Intensive, co-authors with whom I'd eventually be published alongside in this very book, as well as some of Sunny's students. We were all connected and brought together from across the globe to this experience through a universal force that is beyond what you can imagine or explain. How's that for synchronicity?

Abundance isn't something we acquire, it's something we tune into.
—Wayne Dyer

The Process

What I discovered from my own experiences is that there is a process by which, if you trust and follow it, your life will unfold in magical ways. Doors will open, people will be placed onto your path, and golden opportunities will emerge. The process I speak of is not a secret; it's not as if I've discovered some underground knowledge that will change the world. I'm talking about spiritual principles that many use every day and live blessed and abundant lives by doing so.

I've found by applying this process—doing the inner work and familiarizing yourself with the laws of the universe—you can and will unfold the blessings the universe has to offer. Some call it synchronicity, others call it a path of blessings; you may even call it magic or a series of miracles. Call it what you will, but there's a wealth of abundance just waiting for you to tap into it with universal forces at work on your behalf. Once you learn the process, your life will be forever changed.

The process is simple: Do the work, take inspired action, and trust the process.

Do the Inner Work

What do I mean by 'do the inner work'? Simply stated, do what is needed to move forward spiritually, to always be learning, evolving and growing, and take an active effort in the forward progression of your life. For me, that means to always be humble enough to know I am a work in progress, and to be willing to evolve and grow spiritually, to always be working on myself to clear out what's holding me back and heal areas of my life that need attention, and then to take the time each day to get quiet and go within, asking for guidance, and trusting in the guidance I receive.

Just like we clear out the clutter in our homes each spring, we must constantly be taking inventory in our lives and clearing out all that no longer serves us. We must heal unresolved wounds and learn to move forward from situations and habits that no longer serve our highest good to make room for the bountiful gifts that are awaiting us.

Take Inspired Action

As you do your inner work, be mindful of the opportunities that are presented to you, and take inspired action when you receive those nudges from the universe. Listen to that inner guidance when it tells you that you must attend an event, or join a group, even if you don't know why at the time. You never know who you will meet and later collaborate with, and what those connections will lead to in your future. When you get those inner 'knowings' I spoke of earlier, that's the universe guiding you, but you also must be willing to listen and watch for the signs. The universe will deliver opportunity, but it's up to *you* to take action.

How would my life be different if I had not followed that nudge from within that told me I needed to attend Sunny's healing retreat in 2012? Where would I be now? What would I be doing? Would you be reading this book? Perhaps we all would have arrived here eventually, but the path would not have been the same, and perhaps the journey would not have been as smooth.

Trust the Process

I've found the more I work on myself, the more the universe responds and aligns me with opportunities and people who can catapult me forward on my journey. Once I got out of my head and stopped trying to figure everything out, I was able to surrender to the flow of the universe, and trust in the universal laws that everything we need is there for the taking. The universe wants us to be abundant and prosperous; it's our God-given birthright. So it's not enough to just do the inner work, we must also take inspired action. The more we trust ourselves and the guidance we are receiving, the less resistance we will receive. Resistance can act as a roadblock on the path to your dreams. Get out of your own way.

It really is that simple to tap into your life's purpose and allow the universe to guide you. Doesn't that sound much easier than having to figure it out on your own all the time?

When I wrote that chapter in *Living Your Purpose* back in 2012 it was all about finding my purpose and trying to find my way in the world. I knew I was meant for something greater, I knew I was here to do great work, but instead of surrendering to the flow of the universe, I was too much inside my own head trying to figure out a plan, to figure out my purpose and my calling. When I finally gave up the need to do it on my own, and instead started following my bliss and doing what I was passionate about, and listening to those inner nudges from within, that's when my path started to appear. Your emotions are the roadmap to your purpose. Learn to listen to those inner nudges and let your passion and joy guide the way.

What's interesting, I didn't even know it was my path at the time. Looking back, I can see the road I've traveled, but looking ahead, I no longer need to see the path to trust I am headed in the right direction. I now know that by applying these principles and following my bliss, I will always end up where I need to be, meet those whom I am meant to meet, and opportunities will emerge in Divine timing, but first I must do the inner work, take inspired action and accept the gifts the universe is offering. Most importantly, I must trust the process.

LOUISE HUEY GREENLEAF

Author *Louise Huey Greenleaf* has dauntlessly survived the ravaging effects of Multiple Sclerosis since 1981. Despite her confinement to a wheelchair, and battling through the emotional ups and downs of living physically challenged, Louise decided to use her love of writing by sharing her heartfelt words of inspiration with the world, especially to those who live in adverse situations such as her own.

Louise is an award-winning poet and author. Through the years she has been an inspirational and motivational speaker to groups around her community addressing the topic of Living Positive with Physical Challenges.

ACKNOWLEDGEMENT

For *all* who I am, and *all* that I have, I offer my deepest love and gratitude to my Lord and Savior Jesus Christ, for His incessant love and presence in my life always. And to my husband, Don, there are no words other than I love and adore you far beyond definition. I am highly honored to be the one you chose to share your life with. If not for you I would not be. Thank you for literally carrying me throughout our incredible journey together.

DEDICATION

This chapter is dedicated to my superhero loving husband, Don, to our beautiful daughter, Kristen Ruth (Krissy), and to *all* you threads of silk who are crocheted into my heart with love—yesterday, today, tomorrow, and for always.

Connect with Louise

Email: louisehueygreenleaf@gmail.com

Social Media

www.facebook.com/louisehueygreenleaf

www.facebook.com/louisehueygreenleaf/Author

CHAPTER FOUR

Silky Tales of Eternal Grace

By Louise Huey Greenleaf

Grace exists in every moment. Though we each come into this world with our own cross to carry, so too do we hold on to one another with fine threads that are invisible except when recognized through our hearts. When light shines upon them at just the perfect angle, they reveal a magnificent masterpiece created by one single entity whose purpose is to knit, to twist and turn, to weave and braid, to loop and plait, to construct and create into webs. These ties, perhaps metaphorically speaking, represent multitudes of incalculable stories that, even though individual, somehow intertwine and unify us somewhere along the sphere of time and throughout the Universe, urge us meet one another, and another, and yet another. In a second of time, our souls connect to synchronize into one glorious, no longer mysterious, dimension of eternity where time will no longer be counted. Our tales will resonate to inspire God and the Universe as they are all joined together to reveal the long-awaited, all-inclusive, omnipresent, all-embracing, perfectly quilted blanket of love that covers every space imaginable…even far beyond infinity.

Have you ever intentionally taken the opportunity to stop and observe a spider intricately spin its web? It is amazing how it instinctively and rhythmically places each delicate strand of silk in precise order as it continues to work without hesitation, or even the need to rest before its delicate latticework is flawlessly complete. The strands are threads of strength produced by a liquid secreted from the spider's own body, and are stronger than any human being has yet been able to re-create in a material substance. Ah, except when they grow from within our hearts!

I boast to proclaim that every link within my heart represents a meaningful relationship with each possessing its own name. It would make perfect sense that those closest to the center are the ties with long-term family and friends who have been a part of my life, either in its entirety or for a duration of many years. When I look at spider webs, I view them as images of our journeys—yours as well as mine, and the innumerable bonds we build along the way. Who will we meet? What motivates our desires to connect, and how will our stories unfold?

For me, it could seem as though life was destined to be a constant rigorous uphill battle, even before I was born. My parents were still teenagers and already had a two-year-old son when I arrived. The ingredients for my "welcome to the world birthday celebration" were prepared and in place...ready to serve me with a hefty portion of a deflated pink, double-layered conglomeration of chaos, topped with plenty of stress and drama right from the start. But instinctively, like the spider, I immediately began my quest to build a strong and sturdy structure where I could learn to live well. It was through this web that I could survive the forces of damaging mistakes and choices made by those simply trying to do what they thought was best for me, without intending to do harm, yet in truth, had set my journey on a topsy-turvy path of misguided direction. Hey, sometimes life isn't fair, and we get caught up in traps from which freedom seems impossible. But somehow through faith, courage and persistence, we precociously march forward into battle and withstand the tests of time, meeting head on all undesired and unwelcome forces.

Though I cherish each and every relationship in my life, all unique and special in their own way, and as I consider each to be a blessing of monumental value, I must confess that there is a handful that have fully awakened my intuitive senses to the reality that they are part of a master plan that is also my destiny. I believe you would agree that some relationships are nothing short of mysteries and miracles as to how they could have possibly come to be. Perhaps they are invisible threads, perfectly placed by God's very own breath on us. I first, always with my deepest respect, offer gratitude to my maternal teachers for the parts they played in assisting God to set the wheel of my life in motion, allowing that his strategy to bring me to this earth would be carried out in order that *His* glory be revealed—not mine, but through me.

I give thanks to my mother who brought me into this world and gave me life. Although we were not particularly close in ways I had witnessed most mothers and daughters to normally be, and in the ways I wished and yearned for *ours* to be, she did the best she could with the scant degree of skills she had as a teenaged mother. Though her age and circumstances opened questions concerning her level of wisdom to some, I know for certain a whispered thread gently blew in from God and was invisibly placed in her psyche to teach me one of my most valuable life lessons. She taught me to reach for my dreams regardless of the hard work it would take to acquire that which might seem impossible. "Just always stay focused on the prize, Lou Lou, and it will come." Jesus says in Luke 11:9: *"I tell you, ask, and it will be given to you; seek, and you will find; knock and the door will be opened to you."*

I will always believe it was at that very moment she so perfectly wove this strand of God's whir of wisdom into her afghan of maternal love for me, which was then marked with her very own seal of wisdom forever. It wasn't that she lacked the want or desire to give me more; she was a beautiful person who loved God and relied on her angels. It's just that life's circumstances became too overwhelming for such a young woman to juggle. Even still, she grabbed her prize to set on her mantle of eternal history by teaching me a most valuable lesson. That makes me happy for her and for me. Thank you, Mama! Thank you, God!

Thanks, too, to my grandmother, who surrounded me with her wings of love from the day I was born until the day she died. She directed me toward finding my faith in God, and taught me the essential skills I needed to have in order to take care of myself, and one day to care for a spouse and family. I will love her *always,* and I miss her immensely! Thank you, Gramma!

Not a day goes by I don't give thanks to my childhood friend, Priscilla, to whom I was attached at the hip, along with our friend, Cathy. They were best friends who grew up across the street from each other in our tiny country town in Connecticut. We were three girls brought together by way of the cheerleading squad in junior high school. They were a year ahead of me, but that didn't stop us from becoming friends and staying close to one another as we clambered our way through adolescence, facing together the dramatic dilemmas teenage girls get themselves all tied up in knots over. We were inseparable from junior high to high school and into adulthood.

When they graduated, I thought my life was over! Cathy thankfully stayed in the neighborhood, but was busy during the day furthering her education at a nearby school. We continued to see each other, mostly on the weekends as I was still in high school. Priscilla went on to college in Miami, Florida—1600 long miles away. It was hard to stay in touch with her being so far, but when she came home for holidays and breaks, we would get together and carry on as if she had never left at all.

Pris had been gone for an entire year, and was rightfully enjoying her independence as a young adult with new friends, along as well as spending time with a guy whom she had met and fell in love. Cathy was involved with the fellow she would one day marry and I was working at a dinky diner in order to support myself, while at the same time auditioning for singing jobs around my home state in hopes of pursuing my dreams of becoming a Broadway singing star. When I landed a part at a small theater on Long Island, New York, I thought my time had finally come; that I could break free from the dysfunctional chaotic life I had endured as a child. But really, how would I pull this off? I had no skills other than the ability to sing, had no money, and owned an old jalopy car that barely ran. Who did I think I was other than a little girl with nothing who would probably end up *always* having even a lot more of nothing?

In the winter of 1978, Pris called, giddy and ecstatic with the news: Her guy had proposed marriage! Though I would not be a member of the wedding party, which would be taking place in Connecticut just months away in October, she invited me to take a trip to Miami to help her with wedding tasks that included lace cutting for the bridesmaid's dresses. In early August I flew to Miami with a guy I was dating. Though we had planned our stay for a week, I decided to extend my time to help her finish what we had started. The story of Pris and I and our connection to one another can only be due to God's plan, reflecting on how situations and relationships come to be in our lives. Sometimes they are as invisible as where and how far the wind blows.

After my boyfriend left to fly back home, Pris informed me we would be joining her fiancé and his friend that evening. His friend was going to be an usher in the wedding in Connecticut, so I would be meeting him regardless, even if I hadn't taken the trip to Miami. Sounded *great* to me!

When they arrived to pick us up, she was in a back room still getting ready. When I opened the door, standing next to her fiancé, was his extremely attractive, suntanned friend with shiny blond hair, and bright blue eyes. Thirty-seven years later, Don Greenleaf is still, and *always* will be, my loving husband and partner for life. My knight in shining armor, the father of our beautiful daughter, my very best friend, champion and angel sent from heaven!

If you don't believe in love at first sight, just look at us and you will! He swept me off my feet and took me to Miami with him to meet his family. We built our life together after I broke free from my tangled web of twisted confusion. Mere months after we married in November 1979, I fell ill with symptoms of an incurable progressive disease called Multiple Sclerosis. Though the news was shocking and devastating, it strengthened our love and determination to rely on faith as we moved forward with our blessed life. We had a beautiful daughter together whom we loved and raised with our absolute love and devotion so that she would know how to be treated, and how to treat others in return. Thank you, Pris!

Though I gave up my dream of becoming a Broadway star in order to spend the rest of my life with the most amazing man on earth, Multiple Sclerosis would surely have stolen the show whatever my choice. However, the threads of the heart are far stronger; they are impossible to break. Believe me, living all these years with such a monstrous disease has crippled me to the point that Don automatically, without question, lovingly, patiently and proudly also wears the hat, *caregiver*. Thank you, my *Thread of Finest Silk*...my *Greatest Love of ALL*...Don!

I have been blessed to sing in my church choir, as well as countless weddings, baptisms, funerals, and holiday events for the last thirty years. Aspiration fulfilled!

It is awesome how the cyber threads of technology have brought to light just how small the earth truly is. Through information sites and social media, I have realized my lifelong dream to share my published words with the world. As I searched for a way to do this, I clicked on an illuminated angel with silky locks of gold. There she was, with her bright and beautiful smile, inviting me to share my gift and ability to inspire through my stories and poems, so I did. Through her, God chose his words to be heard throughout the universe forever, and I continue to acquire more and more friends who share my common love of writing. Thank you, Shanda!

I am overjoyed with my newfound wealth of love and sense of belonging since I and my three of my four brothers were recently found and reunited, also through social media, by our biological father's side of the family after fifty-three years of separation—from the time I was three years old. That is a miracle tale to be read in my memoir one day. Thank you, Uncle Dennis!

I am blessed beyond words to live in this time and place where perhaps I too may be an instrument in making a difference to someone who needs what I can offer by bringing them relief, peace and understanding. I offer my love and friendship to those I have met only through my computer, but they are deeply planted in my heart.

So just as the highly unpopular, eight-legged creature so commonly creeps amongst us, and we may even wonder why God would create such a hair-raising brute, still, we cannot deny the beauty in the lessons we can learn from watching spiders turn their elegant silky tales of divine grace into melodic songs of love. If we still our souls long enough to watch, it will take its leap of faith, find its support and begin to build something enchanting, captivating and glorious from one single thread into many.

As I have tossed my own threads to the wind, they have miraculously moored to strong and sturdy souls who have guided me in paving the way to reveal my own eternal history made with my opus of love. I marvel at the number of beautiful men, women, children, and even animals who are securely and eternally coiled deep within the fibers of my essence. They exist alongside the words and music of wisdom, compassion, faith, hope, forgiveness, kindness, and love that glisten in our hearts and in unknown spaces we will never reach, as God's golden ribbon spins my own tale, and yours, just the way it was planned, forever and ever...Amen.

"Ask, and it will be given. Seek, and you will find. Knock, and the door will be opened."
—Luke 11:

KATRINA ELKINS

Guided by love and an undying thirst to help others, *Katrina Elkins* seeks to open up discussions of the Spirit. Squelched as a child in a Christian religious cult, she knows the heartache of oppression. Her story brings out the issues we all face at different points in our lives, the light and the dark.

Katrina's dream of starting a non-profit organization to help raise awareness surrounding oppression is becoming a reality. Currently, she is working on her memoir, *Sunny Dawn*.

"I try to understand the trials and tribulations of the human spirit. I want to share my stories with others so that I may help those who are more vulnerable."

ACKNOWLEDGMENT

The opportunity to share my thoughts with the world leaves me in complete awe of the guiding principles of love that emanate from Connie Gorrell and Shanda Trofe. I have immense gratitude for my husband, Bryan Elkins. His passion for life is endless and he is my rock and my foundation. I am thankful for my writer friend who helped me during the revision process. She has an exceptionally trained eye.

DEDICATION

This chapter is dedicated to my grandpa, Milton Nesse. He always told me, "Katrina, you can do anything you want." I believed him and he believed in me. Finally, I must acknowledge my Heavenly Father, God. He has shown me the world and is constantly fanning the flames that light my path.

Connect with Katrina

Website: www.katrinaelkins.com

Social Media: www.facebook.com/katrinajelkins

CHAPTER FIVE

Walk Through the Door

By Katrina Elkins

I heard tales of him whispered on the tongue of my grandpa. Harald Hardrada lived a life straight out of *The Norse Mythology*. Physical strength, wit, and a lot of luck took him to faraway lands living a life that gave him the title of the last Viking Warrior. Battles were a common occurrence, a true fight for survival in flesh and blood. The intrigue of his stories enthralled my family's hearts and minds. Accumulating wealth and then giving it away to stay on his journey was a common theme.

He became the thirteenth Norwegian king and was known as a stern ruler. And yet, he was a poet. A softer side, with no physical prowess needed as he created magic within his brain. His poetry would be among the best of the skalds (a Norse bard). He wooed his future wife, the princess of Kiev, with a poem called *The Song of Joy*.

Drawn to the thought of both a warrior and a poet embodying one flesh, I was captivated. In 2008, I called upon Harald's poetic skill to help me navigate the upheaval of emotion with the news of my mother's diagnosis of lung cancer. I felt led to enroll in a women's collaborative writing class. And in my darkest hours, when anger consumed me and dismay filled my heart, I wrote with the inspiration of Harald and his poetic guidance. Connected to the heavens, I felt him close, even though he was born one thousand years before me.

Walk through the door.

Dealing with the struggle for courage and a fight for clarity, I heeded the call to write. I filled my pages with words that were harsh, sad, and angry. As I contemplated what to say in a tribute to my mom at her funeral, a soft caress, a whisper caught my attention. My grandpa watched from the sidelines on the day we buried my mom. His head was bowed, heavy with grief over burying one of his beautiful children. He later spoke to me about my tribute to mom. "That was the Holy Spirit pouring out of you," he shared.

Three years went by and my writing mirrored a desolate land yearning for the rains. On Christmas Eve, I dreamt a vivid dream about healing, and could sense another door was opening. Words flowed from within me. I wrote for my grandpa as he passed into the heavens, I wrote for myself, and I wrote for my children. Poems, sweet rhythms began to gush out. The words surged from my soul. I wrote in the middle of the night when I could not sleep. I found comfort in my pain when I wrote in the park. I longed for the moments when I could release the magic within me. I knew it was possible to come out on the other side with only a soft caress surrounding my heart.

I wrote for almost a year. Words came in a steady stream and healing gradually began. Continuing to imagine Harald and his great poetic ability, I called on his experience at a women's retreat. I envisioned being encompassed by a soft, rolling wave of compassion from God. For the first time, I saw that all my trials, heartache, and loss were acknowledged and then replaced with the never-ending love from the Spirit. I felt released from the ties that had constrained me. My heart was young again and it flew to the skies, above the trees, and came right back down into my core. It pumped new blood, filled with hope, and without the bonds of anguish. I trusted that a renewed sense of freedom would allow me to face any challenge ahead and walk through the door.

As quickly as the river of expression arrived, it retreated and then disappeared. I was stuck, contemplating light and dark and the wonders of the universe and God. Instead of writing, my focus turned to the upcoming birth of my son and the care for my three-year-old daughter.

During one of the most chaotic times in my life I awoke one morning to a clear vision of creating a kitchen to meet the needs of a growing family. I proceeded as if someone was holding my hand. I made decisions based solely on that dream. A door had opened. The path was laid before me. I acted with a sense of calm within that exuded peace.

I started by saying *yes* to an ad for free vintage 1920s cabinets. I found them posted only minutes after a family had released them to the universe. My best friend's carpenter father-in-law had just moved into town. He, his son, and daughter tore down walls and opened new doorways.

Our early 1900s house was transformed by a vision. The crowning day was August ninth and our walls were forever adorned with a beautiful reminder of love and trust. For on that day, five years before, my mother had taken her last breath. I knew this kitchen was not a coincidence; it was a gift from her to us. This project should have broken us, sent us to our knees, begging for mercy. Instead, I was filled with gratitude and hope that sustained us in one of our most trying times.

After completion of our kitchen I received a call telling me of my father's failing health. Tied to his journey toward the heavens, I fought to maintain balance in my own life. Bound to his undying desire for physical life here on earth, I felt enveloped by his diminishing light and fear. I still could not write.

My husband and I were worn out and exhausted from all that we endured in the daily challenge to stay afloat financially. Each day would have its own tears, joys and struggles. Most days were satisfying in our knowing that we had been blessed with enough food to eat and a roof over our heads. And we shared time together during quiet moments in our remodeled kitchen.

Walk through the door. Come out into the sun.

Summoning the effort necessary for some of the most basic needs became a daily burden. Forced to let go of things that I treasured and had carried around with me from my twenties and thirties was a long and arduous process. On the days I offered up an item to release, I began to feel lighter. Eventually, an ease began to take hold and I felt droplets of gratitude replace the resistance to let the items go. Each new owner gave the beloved item a new start. In return, I learned I could bless someone just as they blessed me with enough money to pay our bills. I felt a stronger link to Harald when sharing his practice of giving away possessions.

During Christmas 2013, my husband embodied everything about Santa when he came through the front door with several bags of groceries. In a moment of desperation, when we needed that food, he knew what he must do. His heart expanded as he had given up one of his most valuable possessions, his wedding ring. The following summer, we celebrated our fifteenth wedding anniversary without our beloved rings. Instead, we were grateful for our love, our eternal connection, and our health. We basked in the warm summer sun and delighted in a glass of wine overlooking a vineyard. A transformation had occurred. In a way, we had gone through a complete metamorphous together.

Four months later, in December, my father became very ill and became unable to care for himself. Compelled to help, we put aside our own holiday festivities. I had not visited my childhood home in seven years since my mom's funeral. Being called "Mom" in that house was heartbreaking and healing at the same time. My two children delighted in the same activities I used to do as a child, sledding and engaging in snowball fights. And yet, I felt an intense sadness within me. My father did not celebrate Christmas, and had not in all the years I have walked this earth.

On that quiet Christmas Day childhood memories of oppression created angst within me. I felt as though it was just another day for my father. Holding onto the image of my daughter singing Hark the Herald Angels Sing as she sat entranced by the beauty of the Christmas tree the previous year had carried me through the day. I tried to stay present, and knew in my heart we were showing my father the true meaning of Christmas—love.

We had answered his call in one of the darkest moments of his life. Gradually his fear was washed away as we filled the house with as much love as he was willing to accept. Over the course of ten days, my father grew stronger, but I became weaker. We had to leave for our home, where we would celebrate the joy of Christmas with no limits on our happiness.

Walk through the door. Oh, you beautiful soul. Come out into the beauty of the heavens and revel in the magic of letting go and being whole.

Trying to write for the next four months seemed utterly impossible. I could not find my grounding, but refused to give in to the old thoughts of not having enough or struggling just to survive. I repelled them and continued to focus on abundance. My writing was stifled, but I waited patiently for spring to arrive. I almost began to lose hope that this stalled writing pattern would ever end. I literally had let go of everything. I was a clean slate. The anticipation I felt for peace in the future was so strong it compelled me to move forward.

My father was still incredibly ill but he continued to plan on leaving for a business trip that would take him halfway across the country. A few days after Easter, a heaviness entered my body and I couldn't function—I simply wanted to lie down. Tethered to his soul, I felt him relinquishing the hold on his body. God called my father home and his spirit was on its way to the heavens. The next day, I had a lightness within the core of my body that reminded me of when my heart fluttered into the skies at the women's retreat. The old journey through oppression was now nearing its end.

Walk through the door. Come out into the sun.

A week later it was time. Seven years earlier I promised myself a stay at the Davenport Hotel as a symbol of closure to a difficult part of my life. It was now April 2015, springtime. We had buried my father that morning in the same cemetery as my mother and my newborn sister whom we lost when I was three. The air was warm, the sky was a crisp blue and I was caught up in a lightness that felt as though I had been resurrected. It seemed I could have swirled into the heavens, tapped into everything that was good in that moment. A realization of synchronicity flowed into me as the hardships washed away and left only the beauty they created within and around me. Completely present and filled with gratefulness, I sensed a new beginning and a new door opening.

My husband and I looked out our hotel window and we could see a couple on the balcony seven floors below us. Immediately I felt connected to the woman and her life. I was reeled in by the expansiveness of her soul. She sat next to her loved one, with a bottle of wine, two glasses, and a view of downtown Spokane—right in the heart of the city. The sun beat down on them and their faces were illuminated in the brilliance of the light. They appeared to savor every moment of the warm spring air. She looked up at us. Her countenance was divine. Drawing us down, they welcomed us onto the stage, and my husband and I were hooked. We could not resist the temptation to join them, and made our way down to the discrete and sequestered balcony.

I walked through the door, and onto the balcony of the universe. Fresh spring air permeated my soul and I was enraptured by the life-giving rays of light. My spark of love and an unbelievable lightness of being felt magnified in the sun's radiance. The magic of God's touch was so present. I was excited to meet her. She greeted me like an old friend, "Welcome," she said. "Come and sit. You look amazing." Her eyes sparkled as if the entire cosmos filled them.

"Of course, it only makes sense," I responded. "We just buried my father today, and a huge weight is lifted."

"You look so light and so fresh, like you have an extraordinary youthfulness," she stated. Her manner was delightful.

With those words a truth became apparent. It seemed to me that she had waited in this spot just to tell me that—waited there for the last seven years. Waited with Harald, God, my grandpa, mother, and my newborn sister—watching my life. Waiting for the moment I would walk through the door onto the balcony, and into the warmth of the sun, creating another layer of invisible thread within my life.

I was touched by the sincere beauty of her spirit. I wanted to tell her everything and yet I sensed she already knew it all. Drawn to her gentleness and obvious joy, I was in awe. A new life had emerged and with it, a new beginning.

And then it happened.

"My husband is a writer," she said, turning to him.

I took pause in the quiet acceptance of those words. "Yes, I am a writer too," I said. "I have a story to tell and I have been stuck for over three years."

"It is so hard to let yourself be vulnerable, to show the world what you feel within," he said.

And in that moment, God showed me that I was not alone in the struggle to show life's challenges through the written word. I entered the doorway and embraced the warmth of the sun, and in turn discovered a friendship that placed me further on my path and connected me to a larger piece within the fabric of humanity.

SHELLY KAY ORR

Shelly Kay Orr is an author and Certified Mind, Body, Spirit Practitioner. Since 2012 she has grappled for meaning to the many questions that her diagnosis of Dissociative Identify Disorder (DID) has presented. The lowest of lows came with an attempted suicide and near-death experience in July of 2014. It was in that moment that the noisy, active chorus in her head became laser focused on the love, unity and oneness of which all of humanity is a part. Shelly has  arrived at this place of clarity with acceptance for the 50+ dissociated identities residing within her and can now share the tools she has developed with others to guide them toward their own hope, love and joy.

ACKNOWLEDGMENT

Appreciation and gratitude to Connie Gorrell and Shanda Trofe for your encouragement and guidance on my writing journey. Sunny Dawn Johnston and Stacey Dean, thank you for believing in me when I didn't believe in myself. You are both amazing women and your love, compassion and encouragement has helped light my way to hope and joy. Thank you to my husband Andrew for your support and love. Gratitude and affection to my sister Renee for her unconditional love and support. Poppy, thank you for being a beautiful light.

DEDICATION

This chapter is dedicated to all the men, women and children who battle dark days.

Connect with Shelly

Email: shelly@shellykayorr.com

Website: www.shellykayorr.com

Social Media

www.facebook.com/shellykayorr

www.facebook.com/survivingoutloud

CHAPTER SIX

My Children Light The Way
By Shelly Kay Orr

My heart was so raw I often visualized ripping my chest open and tearing out my heart. All my husband and I had wanted was a baby to fill our arms. *Infertility* is a word no one wants in their vocabulary. Yet this word filled our hearts and heads on a daily basis for nearly four years. Through it all there was a voice, a nudging from within that told me to persevere. I listened and I never gave up—no matter the cost.

Persevere we did. My husband and I underwent test after test. Our diagnosis was classified as Infertility, Unknown. There was no apparent medical explanation for our childless state. We tried everything the doctors suggested. It drained our emotions and our bank account.

The last recommendation of our doctor was In Vitro Fertilization (IVF). The process of IVF is long and emotionally exhausting. It required me to be injected with hormones daily for several weeks in order to stimulate my ovaries to produce mature active follicles. This results in more than one mature egg being produced during that particular cycle. The eggs are removed from the ovaries in a simple out-patient procedure. Each mature egg is then fertilized in the lab with a single sperm. Our first IVF resulted in retrieval of thirteen eggs with all thirteen of them fertilized.

We traveled out of our home state to receive our IVF treatments. The clinic we chose had much higher success rates than the clinic in our own hometown. Looking out across the city, I could see the fertility clinic from our hotel window. Immediately after my eggs were fertilized I felt at one with my babies growing in a dish. I would gaze out the window and send them my love. I encouraged them to grow big and strong. I loved each of them from the very moment they were conceived. When I learned that one of the embryos had stopped growing, I first grieved for it and then released it.

On transfer day, three beautiful embryos were placed inside my womb. I knew that life was growing inside me. I waited and waited until the day I could take a pregnancy test. I scrutinized every development I felt in my body hoping for signs that an embryo had attached and continued growing. It was difficult to discern if the signs I felt within were from our growing child or from the cocktail of medications I had to take during this phase. Finally the day came for me to take a pregnancy test. I couldn't believe my eyes. I was pregnant at last!

Blood tests confirmed the pregnancy and follow-up appointments were scheduled to ensure the pregnancy was progressing. The numbers looked great and they were within the range of a single baby. We scheduled our first ultrasound. I lay on the table excited to see my baby. Wait, what? "Yes," the doctor said, "you are pregnant with twins and they look great. Come back next week and we will be able to see their heartbeats." Twins!

My pregnancy progressed well. There were no complications and we were elated to prepare for our busy future. We learned we were having a boy and a girl. That couldn't be any more perfect. Their nursery is going to be Dr. Seuss-themed. Their names are Andrew and Kai. Each day I grew more and more in love with the lives in my rapidly growing belly and their constant thumps and twirls.

On May 12, 2010, my life would change in a way I never imagined possible. I had not felt well the previous two days. I scheduled an appointment with the perinatologist. The nurse did an ultrasound and I knew right away that something was not right. Andrew was in distress. There was very little fluid around him. Kai looked good, kicking and squirming. The nurse told me to wait in the examination room and I asked if I should call my husband. She said yes.

Once my husband arrived we waited and waited. When the doctor came in, I knew from his face that were about to receive bad news. Andrew would not survive. His amniotic sac had ruptured and he had very little fluid around him for protection. He would eventually crush his umbilical cord, cutting off his source of life.

Kai was given a ten percent chance of survival. I was told I could go to the hospital and terminate the pregnancy immediately, but I refused. I opted instead to be prescribed an antibiotic and went home on strict bedrest. If I started to run a fever I was to come to labor and delivery triage immediately.

So, I went home. I read everything I could find that evening on this subject in an attempt to save my babies, but…it wasn't meant to be. My fever reached 105 degrees and my blood pressure crashed. I was rushed to the Intensive Care Unit and the doctors informed my family that the babies would not survive, and there was a good chance I would not survive as well. Without Andrew's amniotic sac as protection, bacteria had entered my uterus and spread. I had sepsis.

The next morning, I went into labor and my beautiful son was born still. I had been told that Kai would be born immediately after Andrew, but that did not happen. I went through labor again and Kai was born alive two hours after her brother. My husband and I held her and talked to her. The nurse encouraged me to wrap her tiny hand around my finger in hopes she would squeeze it, but she couldn't. We poured love into her until her tiny heart stopped beating.

Kai had the sweetest baby face we had ever seen. She was beautiful. She had her daddy's long skinny feet. Andrew had my long fingers and cute toes.

A piece of me died that day with my children. A part of my heart stopped beating right along with theirs. I could imagine nothing worse than going through labor and delivery, holding your children, then leaving them in the morgue at the hospital. The next time I would see them would be in the small wooden casket at their funeral.

Persevere. As soon as I was cleared to begin trying to conceive, we started again. We transferred four frozen embryos, but there was no pregnancy. We tried another IVF, with no pregnancy. I was over forty now and my egg quality had hit a wall. I begged the Universe to show me the way. Then, I heard the message: an egg donor.

My husband and I scrutinized egg donor profiles for days. We each read profiles independently and compiled our list. One donor was at the top of both our lists. We had our match. We traveled to our fertility clinic again with high hopes. Two beautiful donated embryos were transferred into my womb and it worked! I was pregnant again with one child. On October 26, 2011, our beautiful daughter Poppy was born, happy and healthy.

From the moment Poppy was born she was a different sort of baby. She was alert and would lift her head in an attempt to see who was talking among those present with her. She was attentive and there was a special sparkle in her eye. We never spoke of the twins after Poppy was born. Someday we planned to tell her about them, but not until she was older.

As amazing as motherhood was, I struggled. My had postpartum depression which escalated. Intrusive thoughts filled every waking moment and often infiltrated my dreams as well. Being a mother taxed my brain. I wanted this more than anything in the world, so why was it this difficult? I wanted to be a good enough mother and felt like I was failing. I would do anything for my daughter and one day I changed course.

During one of my postpartum doctor visits after the twins' birth the doctor suggested we get grief counseling. I followed his advice and established a relationship with a therapist, Stacey. My trust in Stacey had grown over the years but still I held back. Oftentimes there were things I had wanted to say, but didn't. I had showed Stacey only a small part of myself, but my desperation to be a good mother finally overrode my ego. One day I decided to speak up and began to tell the truth about my state of mind.

For my entire life I had convinced myself that everyone had the same thoughts in their mind that I did but no one ever talked about it. There must be some unwritten rule that's never mentioned, I believed. I had expressed my inner experiences a few times to therapists and none of those turned out well. I was willing to trust once more. I was willing to be honest and vulnerable. And so I began to tell my story.

I see things that no one else sees. I hear things that no one else hears. I always have. I miss time, lots of time, years at a time. My mind is a hustling, bustling, vibrant world. People go about their day in my mind the same way we go about our business in the world that we all have in common. In my mind there are conversations, relationships and emotions. Buildings, lakes, streams, forests, carnivals, trains and communities are built in an instant.

Sometimes the people within my mind would take over control of my/our body. This would result in lost time for me. I would often find myself in places with no recollection how I got there, or even why I was there at all. This was normal life for me.

Dissociative Identity Disorder (DID), formerly known as Multiple Personality Disorder, was the diagnosis Stacey gave me. Of course I had heard of it but I didn't really know what it was. As soon as I left her office I Googled it. It fit. I felt relief and then fear. Acceptance and denial. Round and around we/I went for quite some time. What was remarkable to me was not the fact that I had DID, but that other people did not. Other people's minds are quiet at times, I learned. They hear chatter but it's their own voice within. My internal voices are not my own. There are no other worlds inside most people's minds. People have told me it's just dark, black within their mind. I can't imagine that.

I began the difficult work of trying to live in the present. Presence is what I wanted and needed most. I had to be present for me and for my daughter. It was my fight for *presence* that was taxing my mind. It was the internal struggle that led to postpartum depression.

Poppy was going to light my way. I knew it.

Poppy began talking early and she communicated well. Her first word was actually two, "all done." At around sixteen months of age Poppy began speaking of angels in our house including her brother and sister. Poppy also talks regularly to someone named Daisy. Daisy goes with her everywhere and Poppy tells us she is her angel. Daisy is Poppy's guardian angel.

I started speaking to Poppy about the Archangels. She speaks of Archangel Michael often and she knows to call on him for protection. These conversations have become the norm around our house. If Poppy isn't talking about Andrew and Kai, she is talking about Daisy or the other angels that fill our home.

Poppy's love and attachment to the angels and her deceased brother and sister encouraged me to begin searching within for my own authentic, spiritual self. Poppy's light rekindled the light within myself. The innate *knowing* that Poppy was born with resided within me, too. I felt it. I knew it. I needed to know more. I started reading and attended a conference in Sedona, Arizona. It was there that I met my mentor, Sunny Dawn Johnston.

I learned so much from Sunny but one of the most monumental was the day I realized I am a miracle. My mind created DID as a protection. Whenever I experienced trauma that was too great for me to process as a child, my mind would create a separate identity that would hold onto that experience for me. These identities allowed me to live my life as a "normal" little girl. My mind is amazing. My mind is beautiful! I didn't need to wish all of the identities away. No, rather, they needed love and acceptance just as I did. On that very day my relationship inside my head changed and I felt my light grow brighter.

The threads of infertility and child loss led to my daughter Poppy coming into my life. From her came the threads that lead to my DID diagnosis, my therapist and my mentor. The threads wound around each other and held me at times in an embrace when I couldn't embrace myself. The threads in my life formed a web, providing respite when I needed it.

I now add to the threads by reaching out to be of service to others who have DID and those who have experienced trauma. These threads join to connect us all, it's our Oneness. We each make a unique contribution to this unified thread, turning it into a kaleidoscope of color and love around us and within.

VICKY MITCHELL

Vicky Mitchell accelerated her journey of self-discovery after traditional medicine failed to diagnose her son's allergies. In the process, she earned certifications at The Institute for the Psychology of Eating and at The Institute of Integrative Nutrition. She was guided by Sunny Dawn Johnston and others to increase her self-love and listen to her intuition. Her son is now healthy, and Vicky's persistent positive outlook reflects her own mental, physical, and spiritual health.

Vicky's challenges included eczema, allergies, weight fluctuations, and cataracts. Using the right food, attitude, and energy as medicine, Vicky has found a passion for health and helping others and coaches you to identify, achieve and maintain your wellness goals. She would be honored to guide you in reaching your wellness goals.

DEDICATION

I dedicate this chapter to my many invisible threads and all those who support me.

Connect with Vicky

Vicky Mitchell, Intuitive Holistic Health Coach

Email: vicky@vickymitchell.com

Website: www.vickymitchell.com

CHAPTER SEVEN

My Cooking Crew in Heaven

By Vicky Mitchell

My intent in writing this chapter is to increase your peace and joy by showing you that you are supported—even if you are not aware of it. Support comes in many forms. Some may be life altering but many will be subtle, even invisible. These invisible threads can form unseen bonds with our past, and our now-passed supportive loved ones, if we allow them. All of these bonds are gifts from heaven. I believe that increased awareness of, and gratitude for, my many invisible threads strengthens all these special bonds. These connections provide support that helps guide me on my wonderful healing journey of self-discovery called *life*.

In this chapter, I will focus on a subtle invisible thread. I want to share it with you because I have found that as my appreciation of this subtle bond grows, my guidance (and therefore support) gets stronger. Noticing and working with my unseen support has become a skill for me. Just like with any skill, the more you practice it, the stronger it gets. As this skill increases, my joy, peace and inner strength grows significantly because I know my loved ones in heaven are still helping me.

My invisible thread is a connection with my cooking crew in heaven, my earliest teachers—my family. This connection guides me as I follow my passion to bring more joy into the world. I am thankful for my heavenly teachers who help with my calling to assist others in their journey to achieve good health. This attitude of thankfulness is important because our attitude shapes our experiences and how we perceive them. As you make this attitude a part of your daily lifestyle, other areas of your life will become more joyful because you learn to relax and trust yourself—and the Universe.

You may ask why I have chosen to talk about cooking. I know that optimal health begins with good nutrition, just as a good attitude is the foundation of a happy life. In fact, I find life is just one big recipe with one key component—*love*. Not only do I cook with my love, but also with ample love from my cooking crew in heaven. My joy of cooking is in my DNA. My grandmothers and mother were very good cooks and my dad loved to eat! They guide me from heaven to this day. The first way they guide me is through fond memories of their artistry in the kitchen.

Big Momma, a petite southern cook, was my mother's mom. Whenever she was cooking, the house filled with the aromas of her fried foods. The very thought of her cooking makes my ears dance to the tune of food sizzling in the pan. She showed her love by being of service in the kitchen. She fed our souls as well as our bodies. My most vivid memory of Big Momma's most unique skill still amazes me. She was a surgeon in the dining room. After placing the fried fish on the table, she would make an incision and, with one motion, skillfully pull out all the fish bones. This memory still makes me smile. When I fry foods, I know she lends a helping hand. Thank you, Big Momma.

And while we're speaking of fried foods, I will tell you that my mom made the best fried chicken I have ever tasted. She skinned the chicken breasts and placed them in salt water overnight. The next day she would rinse the breasts, coat each one in flour, and fry it. As her mothers before her, the very thought of my mom's frying makes my senses come to life. The crunchy crust was my favorite part! She taught me to make cooking a priority. Thank you, Mom.

My dad's mother, Bubby, also showed love through food. She was also petite in stature and yet another giant in the kitchen. Just thinking of her chocolate cake and twist cookies makes my mouth water today. These treats were served only at holidays and birthdays for they took extra care and precious time. When Bubby folded the ingredients into her chocolate cake, it became a spiritual experience—a gentle, meditative process undertaken with grandmotherly love. Her twist cookies required special care as the dough had to be chilled overnight. The extra time and obvious love given to the creation of these treats made them, and the holidays, most special. Family recipes taught me patience and the art of gentleness with ingredients. Bubby guides me when I make sweet things. Thank you, Bubby.

Memories are the first ingredients in my invisible thread recipe. Another essential ingredient is the love they put into their skills which in turn made each dish taste so yummy. They had pride in their crafts in the kitchen. Like these women, I always include love in my food and have great joy, pride and satisfaction in being in the kitchen.

Now we come to my dad—and the third, fourth and fifth ingredients in my invisible thread recipe. My dad ate with such joy; you could see it on his face. So, the third ingredient is eating with *joy*—whether eating alone or sharing your food with friends and family. Whether it is in life or cooking, I remember to enjoy and appreciate the moment.

He also taught me, by example, to be grateful. He always thanked the cooks. When I really enjoy and appreciate my food, I think of him. In between bites of food, my dad would share his wisdom. He taught me that it is okay to make mistakes. Now when I choose to throw out a creation, I smile and try again. I know if I make a mistake, it is okay. Thank you, Dad.

As mentioned previously, attitude is important. When I get ready to cook, my attitude is love and enjoyment. I was not always as open to these invisible threads as I am today. I learned that three things, being open, aware and taking action, helped my cooking, and my life, go more smoothly. Each of these three are ingredients in my invisible thread recipe.

My very purpose is to have fun while nourishing myself and others on a mind, body and spiritual level. So today, as I get ready to create in the kitchen, I ask for help with openness and awareness. An example of being open, aware, and taking action follows.

I often think the combination of flavors and textures I like and what my cooking crew in heaven would like. For example, when I eat sweet potatoes I think of my mom because she loved them. I steam bake them by washing the sweet potatoes and placing them in a baking dish. Then I add water to the pan until half of the sweet potato is immersed in water. I bake them, covered, in a preheated 350-degree oven for about 2 hours until they are soft to the touch. After they cool, I peel and mash them. My son eats them just mashed because they are moist and sweet. Mom told me to try them with pecans or pecan butter, cinnamon and a dab of coconut oil—yummy!

The next ingredient in my invisible thread recipe is *listening*. Opening the channels of communication is like preheating the oven. Often when I open my spice cabinet, I think I already know which herbs or spices I plan on using. Once I was about to add some other spices to my sweet potatoes but decided to use only cinnamon. I have tried other spices with this dish and did not enjoy the flavor as much. Sometimes I will have a seasoning in my hand and put it back. I question myself—which one should I use? I select another spice or herb and thank my mentors.

Sometimes this knowledge is similar to getting a tap on the shoulder as an idea pops into my head. When this happens, I have to trust the information I received. If I downplay it or ignore what I am told, I would not be trusting and taking action.

In those cases, my lack of follow-through sometimes causes the information to keep coming back to me. For example, I wanted to make a savory and sweet nut and blueberry dish. When I was figuring out which herbs and spices to use, I remembered that oregano helps the body metabolize sugar. Not only is this spice savory, using it made me think of my dad who loved Italian foods, which often contain oregano. I also wanted to use my favorite nut and spice combination of pecan and cinnamon. Cinnamon sweetens the dishes but I did not trust that the cinnamon and oregano would taste so good together, so I Googled my question: What spice/herb goes well with cinnamon? Oregano was not on the list. I doubted my intuition, but then the next morning I somehow knew to use oregano. So, in a food processor I blended together 1 cup pecans, 1 teaspoon cinnamon and ½ teaspoon oregano. Then I mixed in 1 cup blueberries. I liked the taste but wanted something warm so I scooped out some and added a dab of coconut oil and warmed it up in 350-degree oven for ten minutes. I loved the taste, and I thanked my mentors.

You might be asking, "So what? It's just a recipe." Well, to me, how you cook is a metaphor for how you experience life. Do you love yourself enough to enjoy your life by being present and savoring your life and your food? Do you rush through your life, yet stress about the details? Or do you relax and enjoy creating your day or your dish? Do you find the fun in the process of life and cooking? Do you make yourself a priority, including taking time to taste your meal in a leisurely fashion? Are you numb, or do you love your life and food, including cooking? I had not been trusting or open.

When I surrendered and used my intuition, my taste buds were happy. In other words, whether I am cooking food or having another experience, I need to get out of my own way and let life be easy and delicious by trusting, for life is a menu of experiences. I feel my way through the menu choices in life. In order for my cooking crew in heaven to guide me, I have to trust the Universe and myself. For without the key ingredient of trust, no matter how open and aware I am of my invisible threads, I will not act on information I receive. Just as what can happen with fresh fruits and vegetables—my invisible thread could wilt and decay. In contrast, if I surrender, trust and act, then I can create wonderful dishes in my healing journey called life.

So let's recap. Below are the ingredients I use to make the most of my subtle invisible thread, my connection with my cooking crew in heaven:

Memories
Love
Joy
Appreciation
Openness
Awareness
Trust
Action

Remember any recipe is just a foundation or suggestion. The more you understand *your* personal preferences, strengths and weaknesses, the more you can customize your own recipes in life. May you trust yourself enough to grow your many invisible threads and may you awaken your soul's taste buds to savor and enjoy your connections with your loved ones in heaven!

MELISSA KIM CORTER

Melissa Kim Corter has never been one to follow the rules, color inside the lines, or be led by the crowd. Her work has taken a similar path. As a spiritual photographer, teacher, and transformational guide, Melissa helps people release fear, removing emotional amour from life experiences and beliefs. Through various modalities coupled with her heightened intuition, she connects with your spirit for deeper truth and guidance on how to shift limiting beliefs. Melissa enjoys watching the magic unfold with her clients when they begin to consciously create what they desire.

Melissa lives in magical Sedona Arizona with her two fur-babies, husband of twelve years and eleven-year-old son. She teaches classes online and hosts workshops and retreats. Her clients have deemed her the "Soul artist" who captures the essence of who they are and showcases it in her portraiture.

ACKNOWLEDGMENT

Much love to my grandfather, Raymond. The day I lost you began the journey deep within my soul. You brought light and joy into my life; it took me twenty-four years to recognize the gifts you gave to me in your presence. Your spirit continues to guide and remind me that being the "crying child" was a blessing, I embrace my sensitivity and it serves me well, I thank you for that.

DEDICATION

Thank you to my students and clients for showing up. You taught me to love myself enough to show up for me. Kristopher and Jared, you have always been there to hold space for me as I learned and discovered who I am. I love you into the next life.

Connect with Melissa

Email: capture@melissacorter.com

Website: http://www.melissacorter.com

Social Media

https://www.facebook.com/melissacortersoulartist

https://twitter.com/MelissaCorter

www.instagram/melissacorter

Periscope: @melissacorter

CHAPTER EIGHT

When You Show Up for Yourself, Magic Happens

By Melissa Kim Corter

The silver thread, in my eyes, is the connection between our human physical body and Source, our creator, or to whatever the God of your understanding may be. When we access the silver thread within us, we beckon wisdom, insight and unlimited potential. It is when we disconnect from the silver thread that we feel fear and create suffering in our lives. Each of us has the potential to create anything that our hearts desire, yet most never will. It is an unfortunate truth that fear can oftentimes feel so great that it overshadows even the most desirable of our dreams. We can easily become jaded by the world and by our experiences if we get lost in emotion and reaction. The root of this can be traced back to our perspective on those experiences.

There is great opportunity to expand beyond your wildest dreams if you allow yourself to step into that fear. The beautiful thing about the silver thread is when you allow yourself to be connected there is no room for the fear because your attention is no longer placed on generating or feeding it. Connection arises from suspending disbelief, control, and moving from knowing something to *really knowing* it from a deeper level of awareness. My own knowing came from letting go of what I thought I knew and releasing the need for control.

Time and time again I have witnessed the beautiful weaving of spirit into all of my life's experiences. One of the most profound ways has been in the awareness of my own stubborn actions and behaviors. Coming from a place of self sabotage and inner criticism, success could never fully manifest in an organic and graceful way. There was a part of me trying to hold back to create a false sense of safety. When my eyes opened, fully observing how I was engaging in this detrimental behavior, I became empowered to shift it. I learned that there is an art to surrendering; letting go allows doors to open.

When you continue to push (because we like to think we know best) doors close, sometimes even slamming in your face. For some of us surrender means no longer having control, yet did we really ever have control to begin with? There is a difference between personal power and being in control. Personal power runs deep and is within the core of an individual if they choose to access it. Control is usually an action or behavior to force, manipulate, or cause change. Personal power is guiding and directing energy with the understanding that there are other forms of assistance and guidance available as well. Control often stems from an attitude that says, "I've got this; thank you, but no thanks." So why then do we ask for help and turn it away when it is offered? Again, I believe control is the answer—we try to control how the assistance or help arrives. This feeds the ego's desire to be driving the bus of our lives. The silver thread awaits your attention; it never left you behind. It has been leaving little signs for you along the way to remind you that you are never alone and are never separated from Source. It is the belief that there is a separation that causes us to become reactionary or make rash decisions, and it all stems from the lack of trust.

Moving from a reactionary attitude into a consciously creating attitude takes discipline beyond reading the greatness of the newest self-help book or even a week long retreat where you remove yourself from your environment to decompress. These are both wonderful tools and I highly recommend them, yet having the discipline to redirect your attention and thoughts is where your true point of power lies. Self-improvement books may offer insight and instruction, but you have to be the one to talk yourself out of quitting on your dreams when you feel the fear setting in. Your tools can open a door and some will even get you into the passageway, but your own inner guidance and belief in your ability to shift the situation will take you to the other side of it.

This is the place where the magic is waiting to be witnessed and embraced. In the hallway of uncertainty we can choose faith, and it is then that we discover strengths we never knew we had. We uncover the energy needed to press forward. We reveal the true grit, heart, and spirit that has always been there, only latent to the fear and anxiety that has had the louder presence. This is the opportunity to show up for yourself. It takes courage and trust in your spirit to guide you, willingness to surrender, and loving yourself enough to know that you deserve to receive.

Trusting in your spirit to guide you can be as effortless or as grueling a task as you decide it to be. Trusting your spirit is different than trusting the aspect of 'you' that made bad decisions in the past. Let that go and forgive that part of you. You wouldn't scold a child every day for having an accident, long after the incident is over. Stop beating yourself up for old behaviors and learn to love yourself through it. Love not only conquers fear, it gives you permission to recognize that you did the best you could at the time, and if you didn't then, you are committing to doing so now. Love yourself more either way. When you practice self-love, you begin to trust yourself because you are showing up for you. The magic of this universe is not hiding from you or punishing you for having negative thoughts; it is always present, only waiting for your attention upon it.

Learning to love myself has not been an easy journey. I am faced with larger opportunities every day to deepen the love I am cultivating for the person I have become. We can hide from others, we can manipulate circumstances and even get away with it for the most part, yet you cannot hide the truth from yourself. You know when you have ducked out of a commitment or responsibility. Only you know how that sits in your body, how it weighs you down. Each time a choice is made to take action, or in this case, not taking action, there is a consequence. Sometimes it is a positive consequence, such as saying no and feeling lighter because you spoke your truth and honored your feelings. When it is a choice where action was not taken, then it feels heavy in your body or regretful in your heart; you cannot hide those feelings from yourself. This is where many people can numb themselves out of feeling because a choice was made against their wishes, or from a place of not honoring their true feelings. Loving yourself is learning to find ways to begin honoring that internal nudge and making it a priority to speak your truth. Loving yourself is not always easy and can especially be challenging if in the past you have put the voice, wishes, or agenda of others before your own. Shifting into the space of self-love involves the willingness to let others be uncomfortable if that is what is needed to honor yourself. Not everyone will be able to accept these new attitudes, beliefs, or behaviors that you are adopting. For some it will mean they have to let go of the person they were used to, and this can stir up emotions for both individuals.

Showing up for yourself involves listening deeply, taking as much time as you need, and being willing to be uncomfortable. I have had many moments where I resisted change and was dragged kicking and screaming through a phase of my life. I do not recommend going about it in this manner. It can be experienced with so much more ease and grace; suffering is completely optional. When you really show up and do the inner work everything changes. Gifts are found through what once felt like intolerable pain or betrayal. One of my favorite quotes by Mary Oliver is, "Someone I loved once gave me a box full of darkness. It took me years to understand that this, too, was a gift." One of the greatest gifts you can give yourself is letting yourself off the hook for the past and making a conscious choice to be more loving to yourself in the present moment.

The silver thread within each of us is weaved in the ways we allow it to be. Your connection is unique, perfectly designed for your own unique expression of your spirit. The way you receive, process, convey, and listen to your inner guidance is right for you. It can be similar in aspects to others, yet do not compare your connection with Spirit to another. Only you can know if it feels right and if you are in alignment or not.

As you continue down this path of loving yourself more, or even just learning to love yourself for the first time, you will be met with opportunities for expansion and growth. You will also begin to allow the magic of this universe to greet you in new and different ways. Make a promise to yourself that you will open your heart and learn how to receive beautiful guidance and these new experiences. The more often an individual practices and opens up to receive, the more experiences, magic, and spirit will pour into their life. Layers of your past may be revealed, giving you the opportunity to heal them. Stay open to the lessons and gifts, and they will continue leading you through the process of transformation.

You have the ability to decide how you listen to Spirit and can continue to discover more new ways from this bond and connection. For me it started with a feeling because that was the safest way to experience it. It then evolved into knowing, sometimes seeing, and even hearing my own guidance. Now I use a variety of ways to connect and listen, and the messages continue as my life unfolds with a beautiful harmony enmeshed with spirit.

Allow the truth of your spirit, your own perfect silver thread to prove to you that your spirit always knows the truth. The answers are available and there is always an opportunity to show up brighter, more lovingly, and authentically. Hold on to the silver thread within and trust in your strength and power to heal and create change. Let the thread guide you and bring you the solutions for which your heart calls.

In every moment there is truth and love weaved through your being and all you need to do to access it is to *believe in yourself*. The silver thread within each of us is only a thought...a breath...a smile away.

TONI MILLER

Toni Miller decided to take the second half of her life to come into her own and discover all this world has to offer. She loves to read, meet new people, travel to anywhere there is water and is excited to see where the *winds of change* will take her. Her passion is helping others release their fears and to realize just how magnificent they truly are no matter where they are in their life's journey. "I believe we all came here to learn and to pass on that learning to each other," shares Toni.

In addition to her exploration into writing, Toni is an entrepreneur having owned a successful travel agency. She is an energy healer, practicing Integrated Energy Healing, and is a Reiki Master. She is also a Certified Medium and Intuitive.

ACKNOWLEDGMENT

This chapter is dedicated to my wonderful husband and son who have made my life so full of love and laughter. They have always encouraged me to follow my path no matter where it leads and have helped me every step of the way. I love you more than you can know. To Connie Gorrell for telling me I have always been a writer even when I told her she was crazy! And to all of my angelic helpers who keep agreeing with her.

DEDICATION

This chapter is dedicated to all of those who have ever feared *the winds of change*. May you always know that you are the ruler of your own life and the captain of your destiny.

Connect with Toni

Email: tmmiller6711@gmail.com

Social Media: www.facebook.com/tonimiller

CHAPTER NINE

The Winds of Change

By Toni Miller

Like a leaf blowing in the breeze—that's how I always felt my life to be. Fear was the guiding force that the wind would carry me to my next drama, dilemma or mountain to climb. I tried to never move too far in any one direction for fear that the winds of change would catch me and throw me against the next rock and I would have to pick myself up once again. I maintained a steady course as one day turned into the next.

This way of living worked well for me for many years. In my middle-class lifestyle I maintained a wonderful home, a good job, and a great family. My husband, Keith, was and is one of the steadiest men I have ever met. We went to work every day, enjoyed our time off, paid our bills and went about living our wonderful life always knowing that we were extremely fortunate. We never strayed too far, didn't take unnecessary chances and, as I look back now, it was the perfect life for those never stepping out of their comfort zone. If I could just maintain this steady course until I peacefully died in my sleep, I had it made! Don't get me wrong—there were times that the winds of change blew, but never anything that was not easily fixed or handled. I was truly blessed!

I watched the news and heard stories of car crashes, famine, tornados, hurricanes, starving children in Africa but as you can see, I lived in a bubble. *Don't Make Waves* was my motto and hopefully the winds of change would pass me by. If I stayed under the Universe's radar, I might just skate through. Who was I anyway? I was just a tiny speck in the sea of life.

Looking back, fear was my driving force. *Nothing* was done that was not motivated by my fear of change. If anyone even suggested that change of any kind might be in the air, I refused to acknowledge it. Even presidential elections drove me crazy. I wasn't a hermit, though. There were a times that I did manage to step out of my comfort zone because I did not want it known by others how fearful I had become. It was as though I was holding up the world and one false move would send my world tumbling to the ground. Oh, to think I could hold up the world, or even my little piece of it, and stay unnoticed by the Universe.

Growing up I was told that the Universe was run by a God that wanted strict obedience or something awful would happen. Death was the "Lord's will" and we should never question it. Watching the evening news was enough to see that bad things do happen to good people, so it was no wonder that we are all fearful. The big bad wolf does come to the door and Mother Hubbard's cupboard does go bare.

As I now know, the winds of change always blow and sooner or later that which we fear always come to the surface. When the time comes for our lives to shift, whether we are ready or not, it will be time to lay down our fear and directly face what is to come.

Mine came in the summer of 2009 when my boss of almost twenty years retired. I was a fifty-three-year-old woman with no college education and the worse unemployment rate since the great depression. My husband and I, like many people, had bills to pay and were putting a son though college. Finding a job was almost impossible with the country's economic downward spiral at the time. College graduates were over-qualified for the jobs they were forced to take, large companies were laying off long time workers and pink slips were as common as sack lunches. The government was bailing out car companies and banks, but my bailout would be unemployment.

There were many fears at my door but little did I know at the time that only by letting go of the fear of change, by stepping up to be recognized, and not trying to hide from the universe would I be able to gain the wisdom and knowledge to free myself from my biggest fear. When we become attached to 'things' or the way we feel things *should* be we lose who we are.

It is a sad fact that that humans only learn from life when we are faced with our greatest fears. Only then can we see that we are strong enough not only to survive them but how in directly facing that fear we become more than we ever thought possible. What we fear most can and will happen—until we let go of the anticipation of what we perceive to be the worst outcome. I never realized that it was in my power to face this new phase of life with an open mind and with the sense of a new adventure. I had the power to see myself as a victim of my boss's retirement or to see it as a new beginning.

With little prospect of finding employment, I had to face the fact that the only way to earn a living was to do the exact opposite of how I had lived my life up to this point—put myself out into the world and grow my own business. Keith and I have always loved to travel and had visited Mexico several times choosing to stay only in all-inclusive resorts. After using a travel agent a few times, we decided that we could book these trips ourselves just as well...and cheaper. My husband even commented, "Wouldn't it be fun to be travel agents when we retire?"

With the lack of ideas looming, I decided that my strength lied in what I knew—and I knew all-inclusive resorts. So the *'wouldn't it be fun when we retire?'* idea became the only idea that made sense. With a computer and some research, I learned over the course of a few months how to book travel and get paid for it. I signed up with websites for current news of new resorts, had a website for my company developed, printed business cards, registered as a business with my city to become official and, just like that, I became a business owner! I figured that I could sit at home and book travel for people that I knew or for those that found my website. I started with a list of people I had from my job of twenty years. I mailed postcards to let them know about my new business and surely they would call me. I would give them great ideas for the best fit for them and their vacation or honeymoon and I would be making money in no time, all the while straying not too far from my comfort zone of being invisible all from the comfort of my living room.

I can hear you laughing from here! When I was a little girl we lived on a lake. My best friend lived nearby. We wanted to learn to swim, but only by putting one toe in the water at a time. My friend had three older brothers who thought we should learn to swim by being thrown in the water face first! The Universe can be a lot like that when there is a lesson to learn.

Sometimes your lessons come slowly like sticking your toe in the water one at a time, and sometimes the Universe wants or needs you to learn things in a much quicker amount of time and for me, this time belly flop it was!

When my business phone did not ring as I thought it would, I knew I had to leave my comfort zone and get out into the world and introduce myself. After all, they were not going to find me by standing in my living room. I wanted this business to work so I was willing to widen my scope. I knew the minute I made that decision that I was led to exactly what I needed. With nothing but a prayer and lots of nerves, I got dressed up, put my new business cards in my purse and attended a local networking meeting. I had arrived just in time to hand my business card to the event organizer, sit down and wait for my name to be called. I was painfully shy but it soon came to my turn to do what they called an elevator speech. I had three minutes to tell everyone in the room about me and my new business. Those minutes seemed like hours and my heart pounded out of my chest. As soon as the meeting was over I was out of there. As you may know, the premise of networking is that you introduce yourself and your company to the others in the room and if anyone knows of someone that might need your service they will refer them to you.

To say I grew personally that day would be an understatement. I began attending several networking meetings regularly, talking about how I started and what my company was about. I joined the local Chamber of Commerce and went on to become involved in bridal shows. My company took off. I know that I was led every step of the way. Because of my commitment to be willing to take one step in the direction for my company I now realize that the universe helped me find my way. I received opportunities that I still shake my head over and wonder how that came my way. In the first year I was nominated for the Travel Agency of the Year Award by the local newspaper. I know, with all of my heart, that the small step in the direction of my dreams led to things coming together in ways I could never have arranged for myself.

My fear of meeting people and talking with others fell away. I kept stepping out of my comfort zone little by little. I kept saying *yes* and as I did the Universe brought me more to say yes to. I wrote articles and newsletters, never having written more than a grocery list before. I was asked join a committee of a local college as an advisor for those completing business degrees. I was a mentor to new travel business owners and even created an online presentation called *Learn How to Run a Successful Travel Agency*. I tried to be discerning on things that made me feel uncomfortable when I felt it was not in my best interest and I learned to trust my instincts and my guidance to know when that was happening.

"Every change is a challenge to become who we really are."

—Marianne Williams

As I was about to learn, this was only the beginning of the change that was to sweep through my life. It is sometimes only from the mountaintop that we can look back and see how things were set up, not by us, but by forces way beyond our control. You can call it God or the Universe or Source, but as time went by I was able to stand on higher ground to see that my life was a series of synchronicities that was always working in my favor. It really was not change I feared but lack of control that I feared most. I always changed, the world always turned and I met new people. Some people in my life fell away and that was just as it was meant to be, but when I felt like that leaf in the wind I had thought of it as a bad thing. Change was never about how my life could be better by the winds of change. That was one of the lies that I kept telling myself—that change would only make my life worse.

I am not now, nor have I ever been, in control of other people in my life or their circumstances. The only thing I can control is my response to what does happen. When I finally learned that secret, life made so much more sense. The Universe is always multitasking to create new experiences for me. If we can become consciously aware of how we move through our lives each day we encounter meaningful coincidences that help us move forward in a gentle and easy way instead of having the feeling of helplessness.

Look back at any one experience you have had in your life. Was there something that you needed to learn at the time? When it happened, did someone new come into your life that you would otherwise have never met? By doing something I have never done before, I opened myself to opportunities, people and circumstances that would never have come about. I learned that what I thought this little company would become was to be more than I had ever considered. I was looking for an income but the people that would become my friends, the laughter, the learning that would come about for me, I never even considered. I figured that I was there to help others plan their vacations but what I learned from others was invaluable to me in so many ways and everything was give and take. I would help and I would be helped.

Looking back, I realize that I had always had what I needed, even though I had such fears. What If I *always* had what I would need from the Universe in any given moment; could I then give up the fear and know that whatever happens is in my best interest? That is what giving up control is all about. Having control of everything that goes on around me was an illusion, anyway. I was just giving up what I did not have in the first place.

It is clear to me now that life is a series of synchronicities appearing to be random coincidences. These are significant because they point the way to an unfolding of our personal destiny. The more control we can relinquish the more freedom and ease comes with the gifts that life has to offer. My tight control only made it easier to see myself as a victim of life with the winds of change. For me the winds of change were always a storm of circumstances beyond my control when in reality they were the gentle breeze of change that only brought me to another place for my greater good. I now chuckle to myself when I hear others say that they are confused by the seeming random happenings in their life.

I now see events for which I blamed others, the breakups, the arguments, the ending of friendships, the death of my parents, even those winds of change always propelled me into another direction or advanced me forward. These changes were sometimes heartbreaking but always pointing me to the next phase, the next relationship, or the freedom I needed to move on.

We need to be truly consciously aware to watch for the signs and trust that life will lead us in the best possible direction for our growth as humans. Watch and see that the synchronicities in life are a part of the bigger picture, without trying to figure out what it means or where we go from here. We can realize that there is an intelligence in all things that helps us along the way, like a collaboration of fate. This is especially true when we have some of the greatest challenges in our life. We can never know until we stand on the mountain top and look back on things that happened, but we can always know that if we let it, it will bring us to the top to stand in the exact place we are meant to be.

THEA ALEXANDER

Thea Alexander is an intuitive spiritual psychologist, past-life regression therapist, spirit medium, and author. Experiencing psychic phenomena since early childhood, Thea is passionate about sharing her experiences and helping others discover the Divine within. Her work is an integral part of bridging spirituality, the human condition, and psychology. Thea shares her spiritual journey and awareness through writing and teaching.

For over twenty years, Thea has facilitated healing at a soul level by assisting others to develop and deepen their spiritual awareness. Her connection with spirit communicates, with certainty, our soul's journey continues beyond the physical. Knowing, without question, in darkness there is light and in chaos exists the potential for immense understanding.

ACKNOWLEDGEMENT

With sincerest gratitude, I acknowledge my mentor, Sunny Dawn Johnston, for being my light. Humbled by your dedication to inspire, encourage, and support, I am blessed to be in your tribe. I am also eternally grateful to my family, friends, clients, and students for the gifts of soul we have shared.

DEDICATION

This chapter is dedicated to pioneer light-workers who have shone the way through their commitment to others becoming aware of who they truly are; to my soul family, for teaching me how to be human; and, to Spirit without whom the journey would be much less than it is.

Connect with Thea

Email: Thea@Thea-Alexander.com

Website: www.thea-alexander.com

Social Media

www.facebook.com/TheaAlexander

www.facebook.com/InternalFlightLLC

www.twitter.com/DrThea

CHAPTER TEN

Journey to Oneness

By Thea Alexander

Let your mind wander as you relax into the floor beneath you. The here and now fading into the far reaches of consciousness, as you drift backward in time. Sensations of the physical body diminish the further back you go, disappearing completely as your energy merges with the universe. Focus now, on the lifetimes passing by in your mind's eye, each like a silent film. Every muted memory is poignantly alive within you. Knowingness comes fully on-line as your soul recognizes and connects with each moment that has woven the tapestry of your very existence. My first past life regression was an amazing experience. Establishing within me a deeper understanding of my connectedness with the Divine, and proof of the invisible thread connecting my soul with Source.

Somewhere in the level of consciousness that occurs between awake and asleep, I found myself experiencing vivid impressions playing out like two old film reels running parallel in the space on either side of me. I was not a physical body, rather an impression of myself, now in this newly created space. The backdrop was a vast star field that appeared endless. I felt as though I was, for all intents and purposes, walking amongst millions and millions of stars. Yet, there was nothing to support me. No path or trail to follow, nothing but seemingly limitless stars.

The infinite darkness impressed upon me that I was no longer on Earth, and that my soul had journeyed far beyond my physical human condition. I became aware that the films on either side of me had individual frames, and within these frames were scenes that played out within each of them. I glimpsed bits and pieces as they moved by at a moderate pace. Attempts to focus on one particular frame or slow them from passing were futile, and there was a sense of urgency to journey beyond this point.

Frames continued moving by, or rather, the awareness now became that I was moving past them. It appeared as though my thoughts controlled the speed at which things progressed. With this awareness, the films disappeared completely and I found myself drifting toward a large luminescent tube. Glimmering silvery white, mutable density, and in constant motion within itself. My excitement grew, as if de-boarding an airplane to greet old friends.

Finding myself before the great tube, I positioned directly in front of the opening and marveled at how large it was. At many times my human height, it appeared enormous, yet despite this was not looming. Reaching out to touch the glimmering substance, I noted it was cooler than the surrounding atmosphere and it imparted energy that was light and dense at the same time, unlike anything I had ever felt.

I began repositioning slowly into the tube, aware of the energy change within me. My vibration increased substantially and now matched that of my surrounding cocoon of light. Advancing through the tube, slowly at first, and then accelerating at great speed, the tube had numerous twists, turns, peaks, and valleys, as it carried me far away from my Earthly existence. As I traveled, I was able to see through the veil of light and was impressed with the vastness of the star field and the universes laid out before me.

As quickly as it began, my transition ended. The tube ceased to exist, as if it was never even there. I peered into the darkness to detail my surroundings. Met with a vast and seemingly familiar cold darkness, believed myself back where I began. Admittedly, this was an immense letdown. I had feelings associated with a long awaited homecoming, and found nothing in its place.

Pondering, briefly, how incredible the whole experience was I became aware of an immeasurable shimmering silvery-blue light in the distance, as if I was viewing a metropolitan area glowing on the horizon. I became excited, gleeful, and almost giddy at the sight. As it moved steadily closer, the light grew in intensity and I became almost overwhelmed with excitement for no apparent reason. After a moment, I was enveloped in an indescribable light energy. Before me were hundreds of silvery-blue iridescent entities appearing to mimic a loose human form approximately four feet in height. Without distinct features of any kind, there were no fingers or toes, no facial features, no genitals. They had the most glorious energy and an incredible means of communication, telepathy and thought forms.

Suddenly able to communicate telepathically, I received an impression of many joyful greetings and an overwhelming sense of belonging, akin to coming home and being missed as if absent for lifetimes. Of The Collective gathered here, one entity came forward to communicate. I immediately got the impression of my father's energy. Thought forms exchanged between us at lightning speed. Lifetimes of information relayed in seconds of communication. Impressed upon me were significant events from this incarnation and better yet, specific individuals who were now in spirit, all of who had come to greet me. Some stood out more than others, yet all were sending positive and radiating energy.

Instructions from the facilitator played into my awareness, "As you travel backward in time, review the lifetimes you have had. Seek a past life to explore where you experienced the feelings you have had in this one." Rather than a focus on any negative connotation, the intent was to connect and gain awareness of what was brought forward into this lifetime from one passed.

Again, thought form exchanges of communication ensued between the representative entity before me, as it moved ever closer. Now immediately before me, I recognized there was a familiarity with this entity, a knowingness and closeness that spanned more than this moment, more than one human lifetime. Our togetherness was infinite. Bursting with a sense of love and belonging I never knew existed, I felt humbled that the energy chosen to greet me was one I have been with for eternity. Sensations of belonging and an unconditional love, beyond measure and almost palpable, surrounded me.

The main entity and I communicated back and forth for a short while. Others with whom I had incarnated during this Earth life, now in spirit, chimed in, doing so in a manner I would recognize, generally with the impression of their once human voice or a familiar image. Numerous energies came forward in this manner, one after another, presenting with an immeasurable loving presence. I was fascinated by each of them. Every communication was facilitated through an effortless positive exchange of energy.

As the exchanges took place I became aware the entities knew of my purpose for regression, and we agreed my primary objective was to experience, in spirit, the predominant underlying theme central to my emotional existence in human form during this incarnation

Completely trusting of our universal oneness, the lesson began. The main entity, I believed to be that of my father, came forward and blended its energy with mine. The intensity of this experience pales by the sheer lack of vividness of word our language affords to describe it. I will, however, endeavor to be as descriptive as possible. As the energy surrounded me, I perceived warmth with fullness such that it created an unwavering sensation of calm that completely permeated me. The lightness of the energy was surprising, given the immense density with which it enveloped me, feeling like an invisible blanket.

There was a knowingness of our universal oneness, so expansive that it is beyond comprehension. The oneness instilled awareness of universal consciousness, all being of one, connected and thus all knowing. Looking back, I would have thought this to create fear. But it is without fear and only through unconditional love the understanding of all is created. No judgment or seeking to understand, for that is a human condition, only knowingness and acceptance of what is, as it is, and the awareness that it is as it is intended, much like our psychological perspectives on radical acceptance, only much deeper in concept and reality.

The other energies now joined, one by one, until those most familiar to me and I had merged. Completely encircled by them, we exchanged energies, raising the vibration even higher. The remaining hundreds then surrounded me. I was literally buzzing with energy and radiating unconditional love. In unison, we raised the level of our energies. The sensation of completeness, the breadth and depth of unconditional love I experienced filled me through and through as if I would literally burst, yet there was room for limitless expansion. My being had no limitations. The love energy moved through me, within me, and around me. I radiated love and took it in from the energies around me. I was one with the universe, an infinite and expansive being of unconditional love. This was the sensation I yearned for and had been in search of my entire life. I had achieved oneness with my soul family, my tribe, and at long last, I was home.

Several moments passed in this blissful state, and I had already determined that returning to the human condition was not desired. It became apparent to me now why souls do not possess full awareness of our origin when we incarnate. This was too good, too incredible to be without. Unattainable in human form, the sensations of warmth, fullness, calmness, and undulating waves of love would be too much for the human condition to experience for the energy would short-circuit the physical body's nervous system. In spirit form, however, this was intensely incredible and the norm. It was then I realized transitioning to spirit was nothing short of miraculous. The sensation of unconditional love in spirit exists at a level unfathomable by the human condition.

The intensity was broken when the main communicator reminded me of our purpose. We again exchanged thought forms, agreeing we must now create the human condition's experience. Contrast and comparison as was the intent of this regression, and but one of my soul's many lessons.

In unison, the level of energy was gradually decreased and the entities moved away. Remaining in a circle around me, to provide a sense of security and support, the entities continued to move further and further away. I was continually reassured that everything would be okay and that this was merely a representation of my Earth bound experience. They all sensed my apprehension, fear, and ensuing sadness. Several of the entities, closest to me during this incarnation, remained near yet now completely separated their energy from mine. Being in their presence and unable to sense their energy created a chasm one thousand times the size of the Grand Canyon. The physical proximity was one thing, but the inability to mingle energy left me feeling desperately cold, alone, without purpose, and completely disconnected, all too familiar, yet alone with an intensity much greater and unlike anything I had ever endured in human form.

I began to sob. Intense sadness welled from deep within me, and overtook my human form. Sobs from a place so primal, I feared what may come next. My body wracked with an intense emotional pain so great that I wept uncontrollably. With every ounce of my being, I sobbed. For all I never achieved, for all I had lost, and for those who had transitioned to spirit before me. I wept too, aching to remain with them. From the depths of my soul I experienced the loss of my tribe and the intense yearning I had to reconnect. Worse than any loss experience of my human existence, the intensity of this moment far surpassed anything I could have ever imagined.

After what seemed like an eternity, the level of energy returned, moderately at first and gradually increasing to create a state of euphoric unconditional love. The warm sensations of fullness, calmness, and love enveloped me once more with the familiar and welcomed density only their energy could create. The main entity came forward, comforting and consoling me. I received reassurance from many of the souls present that we completed our objective and that I did well with the process. There was nothing but pure, unconditional love radiating around and through me.

As I became aware of the need to return to the present, parting thought forms were exchanged. I felt a sadness stirring in me as I moved back into this space, now knowing there was so much more. The entire regression spanned approximately 50 minutes, yet felt like lifetimes and a split second, all at once.

In the days, weeks, and months that passed following the regression, I felt the same yet undeniably and subtly different, left with a deeper sense of what I am and forever changed. My understanding of the human condition, of soul, of what it truly means to live, expanded exponentially as if I was viewing my life and the self for the first time, only this time from the perspective of soul. I gained a better understanding of my soul, who I am underneath the human condition, and my purpose here. I was unable or unwilling to view my current existence and the concept of 'life' the same way. My thirst to learn more was unquenchable.

I continue to channel messages from The Collective, sharing the guidance I receive with others, as directed, for their messages are not solely mine, but for us all as we share a oneness with the universe. I trust, implicitly, that the universe will reveal answers and experiences, as I am able to comprehend and make the best use of the awareness afforded me.

DAJON FERRELL

Dajon Ferrell is an Army National Guard veteran who served for thirteen years. After experiencing her own struggles with Post Traumatic Stress Disorder due to military sexual trauma she worked toward healing and discovered a path of meditation over medication. Seeing a need for holistic healing modalities in the veteran community, Dajon created Operation Synergy, a non-profit that provides veterans with mindfulness training to help restore and empower them so that they can create a healthy and purposeful life. Dajon also uses her experiences to facilitate workshops, classes, and exercises to help others shift that accompanying victim mentality to one of liberation and empowerment. Committed to serving the veteran community, she also volunteers as a Peer Support Group Facilitator and Peer Mentor for Wounded Warrior Project. Dajon lives in Mahtomedi, Minnesota with her five-year-old son, Logan.

ACKNOWLEDGEMENT

Thank you to Sunny Dawn Johnston for being my mentor, teacher and soul sister! You mirrored the Divine light that I had within me all along. I love you! Thank you to my family, who supported me even when I was a stubborn Scorpio. I love you! Thank you to Logan, my little partner and teacher. May we continue to give each other wings. I love you! Thank you to Mike, for unconditional love. I love you!

DEDICATION

This chapter is dedicated to all those souls who think they're lost. Only love is real, dear ones. May you shine your light bright!

Connect with Dajon

Email: dajon@dajonsmiles.com

Websites

www.soulebration.club

www.dajonsmiles.com

Social Media

www.facebook.com/dajonsmiles
www.twitter.com/dajonsmiles
www.facebook.com/soulebration

www.facebook.com/dajonsmiles

CHAPTER ELEVEN

Connecting Through Compassion

By Dajon Ferrell

Many people classify themselves as introverted or extroverted. I always struggled with choosing one label because I feel more like an extroverted introvert. I love to be at the party and surrounded by great friends, but I also like to sit back and watch a lot of times. In the past, I created the habit of leaving without saying good-bye to everyone. It was not because I didn't care, but more because I did not want to draw attention to myself and really just didn't like goodbyes.

Growing up, I experienced a lot of moving and staying with many different family members. I was used to people coming and going. Saying good-bye at a party reminded me of that little girl just wanting to stay in one town or just be with a particular family member. That same little girl was scared to be seen because she was the reason her mother was held back in life. I was a social butterfly when in a safe space, but at a birthday party I became easily overwhelmed and felt invisible. After more than thirty years of yearning to be seen and expecting others to affirm my value, I finally had a wake-up call. I'll set the stage for how I got to the point where I finally became sick and tired of being sick and tired.

Many people had expected me to have children at a young age, like my mother. Many people didn't realize it but I had experienced physical, verbal and sexual abuse growing up, so being intimate with a boy was not appealing to me as a young adult. In an effort to find my self-worth, I decided to challenge myself and joined the U.S. Army. This came as a shock to many, especially my mother. We were raised to hug trees and were not allowed to play with water guns, because they were 'too violent.' She cried when she first saw a picture of me in uniform. "I raised you to be a strong and independent woman and now you've gone and joined the cattle heard," I remember her saying.

So, here I was, married, just recently given birth to my amazing son. My husband and I had just purchased our first home and were finally planting roots six long years after meeting on a deployment to Bosnia. After those years of yearning for stability and a family, I had finally reached my destination. You know how it goes—you live and live for this big huge destination, not paying much mind to the magical journey you're on each day. If you can just make it to that destination, it will be all good, right? So why did I feel so empty? Why did I loathe the commute I made to work each day?

As much as I loved my little guy, I often felt alone. His dad was a pilot and out of town half of the month. I struggled with a little postpartum depression and had my son in November in Minnesota, which meant we were house-bound during the long dark days of winter. An opportunity came to participate in an international training exercise and I jumped at the idea of exploring another country, another culture, and something that was different from my new existence of being a mother.

When I arrived I felt like my old self again. My job in the military is to photograph the soldiers and write stories to share with media outlets and the public back home. I was excited to be on a new adventure...then the night that rocked my world happened. It took me back to the days of being the little girl who was abused. The teen girl who was raped. The young woman who lacked self-worth and sought attention in the wrong places as self-validation for her existence. The stability I had come to know was now tested at every level.

I was covering a VIP dinner where our leadership met with the foreign leadership. I was given a ride to another base where the dinner was held. The evening was an easy mission as many important people shook hands and exchanged gifts. As the dinner concluded, my leadership exited with our general. The plan was for me to ride back with the foreign public affairs team, but their general started speaking to them in their native language. He informed me that he would get me back to base because the public affairs officers were being sent on a different mission. I was annoyed because it was late and I wanted to get back so I could prepare for a busy schedule the following day but he continued to drink as the band played on. When it came time to leave I hopped into the back seat of the general's car and he sat in the front passenger seat as we began the journey back to base. We made small talk as I told him about my son and husband and he spoke of his journeys to the United States. The car rolled to a stop as we pulled through a small village.

The town square was dark, except for a little bar. The general wanted to stop and see if his friends were there. Once again, I only wanted to get back to base but I didn't want to be disrespectful. Foreign or not, he was a general! As we stepped into the bar, he spoke in their language and ordered two drinks. I had a busy day and was quite tired so I was not interested in drinking. He drank my drink. I still wasn't nervous at this point.

As we exited the bar, his driver pulled up. I entered the back seat again and he slid into the back with me. I couldn't get all the way over to the other side as there was a box on the seat so I had to sit in the middle. Almost immediately, he put his arm around me. I froze. As he began to kiss my neck, I tried making eye contact with the driver. He turned the radio up and repositioned the rear view mirror. I knew at that moment that he had done this before. What was I to do? I was in a foreign country, in the middle of the night, with a foreign official. The stench of his drunken breath grazed my face as I closed my eyes and began to cry.

"You know you want it," he whispered in my ear. No, I didn't want it. He was older than my dad; he knew I had a family at home. I was no longer a mother, a soldier or a daughter. I was a piece of meat. I was something to be taken and tossed aside. He grabbed my hand and placed it on his penis. "You like that?"

NO! I was shaking and crying. I thought to myself, *you're forcibly placing my hand on you. Does anything about this say that I want to do this? Do the tears make you feel powerful? Do they seem inviting to you?* Why was I frozen? Why didn't I kick and scream?

As we approached the gate to base I wanted to get the gate guard's attention but of course we flew past him. We were in the general's car, so no need to stop. His driver parked the vehicle and the general immediately released him. I started to gather my things as quickly as possible. He asked me to come into his cabin. What the heck was going on in this guy's head?

I told him no and that if I didn't get back, people would start looking for me. He said that he would explain I was with him and repeated his *you know you want it* line. He said he would give me a ride back though, for some reason, I was still scared of him. Not wanting to piss him off, I agreed to the ride. I knew where we were and figured I could jump from the vehicle if need be. He pulled over just past my cabin and made one last attempt, but I ran for it. As I navigated the dark steps into the woods, I heard him peel out.

I was not going to tell anyone. After all, I was not actually raped and I did not want a mark on my stable career. But I finally opened up to a leader in my section. He said I had to speak up. I started thinking about what I would do if a fellow soldier was hurt by this man. What would happen if she was drinking or if he was more forceful? What if she didn't get away? I would have felt very guilty—so I spoke up.

Some people gave me shit for "messing with the partnership," though I was supported by my leadership and general. They listened and helped me navigate the divorce that followed, for I returned home to a husband that could not comprehend how a general would make a move like that without me giving him some sort of reason.

So, now that you have a little back story, I'll share how I am where I am today. What helped me weave my story into that invisible thread that connects us all together?

A few years later, I had found a new normal. I was no longer a wife but had found some stability on my own—just me and my little man. Everything was going well until another experience sent me over the edge. This time there was no physical contact in this situation but the outcome left me in a dark and jaded place. What's relevant now are the repercussions that followed. Leadership treated me like an outcast and some of my trusted public affairs co-workers turned a blind eye. Within one month I went from being awarded by the commander to being singled out, feeling like I was going crazy. I was just another number to be replaced. I became a shell of myself, leaving work in tears and going home to lie in a puddle on the couch as my son tried to get me to play with him.

I began to feel that Logan would be better off without me. I was holding him back with my negative energy. I was not the mom he deserved. If I were gone then his dad would be free to move, as he always wanted. No more grieving. No more debt. No more sadness. No longer being a good soldier receiving awards for my work. I felt like my leadership and co-workers would not miss me—they would be more annoyed by the paperwork they'd have to fill out after I died. "Dajon is still a pain in our ass, even though she's not here anymore," they would say.

One night I ingested a cocktail of various pills that I had received from the Veteran Affairs Medical Center (VA) for the post-traumatic stress disorder I suffered after my encounter with the general. I took several pills and then took more. I waited to feel nothing; I wanted to be numb. The Vicodin would numb me while the trazodone would put me to sleep. I sent my brother a text message. I was scared. He called my best friend who showed up and took me to the emergency room. The nurse asked what I had taken and the doctor peppered me with life-changing questions. "Did you try to kill yourself? Do you want to die?"

Wait! Was this what my life had come to? Had I *really* decided to give my power up to people who could not care less? That's when it hit me...*I* was the one who could not care less. I was the one who had given up on me. They were just mirroring my beliefs back to me. They were my teachers, whether they were aware of it or not. I had given up on my self-worth and they mirrored that back at me. This was not about them.

The day I returned to work, we all attended a briefing titled "How to Understand Sexual Predators." A month later they tried to fire me. I was sequestered to a room and reported there each day, sitting by myself. If I focused on the destination in that moment, I would have driven myself crazy. I had to be present in each moment and get through one day at a time. I dreamed of a perfect job that could replace this one and free me. I needed to stick through the process and appeal their decision. I took leave and attended Sunny Dawn Johnston's Mind, Body, Spirit Practitioner course. She helped me start to peel back the layers to see my purpose and believe that I did have value!

In the end, my voice was heard. I stood up for myself and the verdict came back. The state leadership offered to move me back to my old job and apologized for the actions of the others. By then, I knew that I had a bigger mission than being in the military full-time. I needed to connect with others who had similar experiences. I realized that all of the perceived judgement and hate I felt was a manifestation of my own self-sabotage.

All of the abuse had a higher purpose. It did not happen to me, it happened for me. I knew in my heart now that only love is real. All the rest is an illusion. The frustrations we see in others are disowned dark parts of ourselves. It was time to stop the judgement of myself and my experiences and become a witness.

Through meditation, I replaced the VA-issued medication. I endured exposure therapy to 'desensitize' myself from the traumas so that I might help other female veterans. It was time to peel back the layers. No more bullshit.

> *You can't bullshit the Universe.*   —Sunny Dawn Johnston

These words rang true in my heart. I grew to be a more vulnerable and transparent human. I connected with others through compassion. We all have our traumas. We are all here learning, growing and expanding together. We can choose love or fear every day. What will you choose?

> *When the whole world feels so lonely, so cold that I cannot feel.*
> *I remember the message you sent me, that only love is real.*
> —Only Love Is Real, by MC Yogi

You are not a victim to circumstance. You are Spirit embodied. You are here to shine your light bright and to expand those beautiful wings of yours. What story are you ready to release? What part of you have you been holding down? It's now time to rise up. When you speak your truth, you empower others to do the same. How can you step into your purpose by reclaiming your power?

I have started a non-profit to help other veterans who are struggling with post-traumatic stress. I don't want anyone to ever feel like I did the night I took those pills. My goal is to have a healing center that operates on donations. I volunteer with Wounded Warrior Project and I am using my story and voice to connect with others. The heart trauma that is experienced in the military is part of that invisible thread by which we are all connected. I am sharing that awareness within the veteran community.

My advice is to speak up, rise up! Your story is important. It's not about whether you're a good public speaker or where you will share your story—just share it. The connection you spark could be someone's light through their darkest time. It is not about being good enough or knowing enough or being perfectly healed. It's actually not about us at all, but the greater whole.

Be the change that you want to see. Start today! Share your stories as a way to connect through compassion, but leave them where they belong, in the past. You were meant to shine, dear one. Shine on!

TONIA BROWNE

Tonia Browne is an author, presenter, teacher and coach. As a qualified teacher, Tonia has worked in the United Kingdom and internationally for over twenty years. She is a strong advocate of inviting fun into our lives and encouraging people to see that there is more out there.

Tonia encourages self-acceptance and her writing is interwoven with spiritual insights and personal anecdotes. She hopes that her stories can inspire others who are facing challenges or similar experiences.

ACKNOWLEDGEMENT:

Thanks to my mum and dad for giving me the gift of life, to my friends and family who dance with me through this big adventure and to my sister and closest friend. In addition, a big thank you to all those who helped me with this chapter and have made this book possible. A special thank you to my husband who has encouraged me to write and gave me the gift of time.

DEDICATION:

This chapter is dedicated to those who sense and feel more than just this physical realm, and to those who believe us when we share—thank you.

Connect with Tonia

Website: https://time4tblog.wordpress.com/

Social Media

Facebook: www.facebook.com/Time4Tonia

Twitter: www.twitter.com/ToniaUae

CHAPTER TWELVE

The Gift

By Tonia Browne

Synchronicity

Sometimes you are lucky enough to know from experience that there is more to this world than many people have led you to believe. Sometimes you are given a sign, an experience so profound that it changes you forever. It allows you to consider and accept that there may well be invisible threads joining us all. Others may dismiss your experience. They need to feel more of their own to fully accept. You may also be ostracized by some for sharing. It may cause too much discomfort for those that have invested so much in their own belief of reality, so beautifully confined to this time and space. Yet if you accept, or if you are unsure, let the threads of this story tug on your heart strings. Let it help you open to the expansiveness of all there is. By accepting, we realize that we are never alone and we are always loved.

There may well be a Pandora's Box, not of truths to be scared of and hidden, but of beauty, love and hope. Too many of us have been quiet for too long. More are sharing now as the threads interlink and urge us to dance and play together. Sometimes you need synchronicity to give you that final nudge of action. So, today I share with you—The Gift.

Visible Veils

As a young child I did not see a veil blocking our reality from another. I would often *see* or maybe the word is *feel* things that many people did not. It is hard to use a word to best describe it. Some of it may have been imagined but most, I believe, were not.

I could tell which people had hearts of gold yet were misunderstood, like the old man we called Mr. Chips who lurked in the bushes by the park. And those that were given credit but who had unacceptable intentions such as the swimming coach who taught us after school. Many of these feelings came to fruition with newspaper evidence supporting the predictions of a child. I also had the experience of being with someone and sensing their body saying goodbye. It was not sad at the time but I would know it was the last time I would see that person alive. It was always sad later. Initially those close to me would get annoyed with such morbid sharing. In time, however, they would take note if I gave such information as the proof had too often come to pass.

I cannot do this on demand nor have such experiences been consistent in my life. There are phases when it happens and years when it does not.

Many of us have shared stories of loved ones appearing to us after they have died. My mother, for one, awoke early one morning sensing her father close. It was dark and she had awoken from a deep sleep. Initially dismissing it and returning to her slumber, the phone rings and she learns that her beloved father had indeed passed over. The threads of their love, it appeared, were so strong that they connected at his departure.

I remember as a student being shown a lovely property to rent only to see a man standing in the top bedroom, just staring. I knew I could not live there and shared my discomfort. The property had come available as the last resident had died suddenly in the upstairs bedroom. I believe that it was the dramatic nature of the event that had caused connections between the man and the building. Although I had experienced visitations before, being followed and actually shadowed consistently for a period of time was something new to me.

The Meeting

One day my Headteacher walked into my classroom as I was teaching, closely followed by a stranger. I had not seen her before and I looked to my Headteacher for an introduction. She was a parent of a child in our school. She had volunteered to help in our class once a week. The Head nodded and then left. She was chatty and jovial and the children liked her.

She would talk about her life and brought in photos of herself in years gone by.

The Contract

The parent asked if she could help out more often than once a week. I remember asking her what days and times she was suggesting but she said she could not say. I recall so specifically staring at her and time standing still. As the teacher responsible for a class, it was advantageous to know in advance in order to maximize the benefit of another adult for the children. I remember thinking that I did not want her coming and going when it was convenient for her in case it was disruptive to the class. It was, however, almost the end of the school year and there was something in her look that told me to trust her contribution. We talked about tasks she could do if she arrived at the classroom and we were in the middle of a lesson. She smiled.

Mostly I knew when she would help out, but there were occasions when she would just arrive and happily sat sharpening pencils or tidying the books on the bookshelf. Then one day she left and did not return. It was the last week of the school year and we were extra busy with concerts and so forth. I remember asking where she was and was told she was ill. The school year ended and the summer holiday commenced.

The Coincidence

There are times that events happen and you chuckle at the coincidence, yet how many signs, how many coincidences does it take to stop and open your mind to the idea that there is something *else* going on? How many times do we put our faith in the randomness of events, leaving no space for the magic of synchronicity?

The new school year began with a new class, new parents and new staff. I was asked to cover a playground duty for someone. This request also happened on the very day and time that a student in the upper school came to join us on the playground for her service experience. This girl came to me and told me that her mother, the lady who had helped in our class, had joined the angels last night. I was shocked. I had questions. I looked around again to give my condolences but she had run off into a crowd of playing children. A child came to me with a grazed knee and the playground bell rang.

The rest of the day was taken up with the joys of teaching, enveloped in the energy and enthusiasm of the very young. Just being with them grounds you in the now. Their needs and their vibrancy can be invigorating.

It was only later that the student's mother's story unfolded for me. She had been ill—very ill. The day she did not come back into the classroom was the day she went to hospital where the treatment to make her comfortable had been started. I wondered if she had known all along that her time was limited, but she wanted no goodbyes. Could it have been an unconscious knowing that she responded to, a need to be with the vibrancy of the young when her own energy was depleting? There is a power we all respond to far more than we may acknowledge.

I often think of the coincidence of her daughter and myself being in the same place at the same time for that exchange of information.

The Following

Over time, the lady remained on my mind. It was understandable, but I could not shake the feeling I was being followed, as if someone was walking fast behind me to catch up and then would nudge me to say something important. I felt it was her. I dismissed it as me being silly. Days turned to weeks and I could not shake the awkwardness and discomfort I felt. There were often times I would be startled and after a few weeks I felt I was in serious need of some ghost busters. I shared my feelings with a good friend. She said I should just talk with the lady.

One morning whilst I was in the bathroom cleaning my teeth I felt her presence again. Annoyed, I asked her what she was doing and that I needed her to go away!

The Gift

She told me she wanted to thank me. I felt agitated and told her I did not want her following me especially into the bathroom. She explained that she did not see reality as we did. It was not about bodies or the physical environment. It was just soul on soul—her heart connecting with mine. She said it was similar, such as looking through the eyes of a loyal dog. Dogs do not often care where you are or what you are wearing. They are just happy that you are there.

I felt confused. If she could read my soul then she would also know that, although I appreciated her help in the classroom, I had not really considered her a friend. I was uncomfortable. She laughed and explained it was not like that either. It is not what we do or how we feel; it is our soul contracts and I had fulfilled mine for her. I had allowed her to be with the optimism of the young when her body was failing. She had felt optimistic, useful and normal right to the very end.

She informed me that she would leave me if that was my wish. She had not wanted to make me feel uncomfortable. She wanted to thank me in the only way she knew she should. She said it was her gift, her contract. She put her hands out and it was as if the whole room, including myself, were transported into a different dimension. The invisible air became golden light and my whole body felt like my heart would explode with pure love. Then I felt as if it did and I became part of everything. I had never felt anything like it before. It is hard to put it into words and it lasted for only a few moments. My world came back as suddenly as it went. I was alone. I shook myself and reflected. If this is what it felt like when you made your transition, even if it were only one percent of the love I felt, it was an amazing experience. I had almost not wanted to come back. When I focus, I can feel it again. That was her gift to me and I felt her leave me with peace. She had shared her side of the agreement. She knew in time I would share it with those that needed to know. I still think about it—a time shared, until now, only with close friends.

Stacking

Sometimes life is about seeing exactly where you need to go next and at other times you need sign after sign to get to the path you agreed to walk. It is funny that as I sit and write this chapter, I become even more aware of what was stacked up for me in the way of signs that I had consciously missed until the very moment of typing. It is as if the penny had dropped and the road map was so obvious and carefully constructed. If only the map had been visibly in my hand before, maybe my route would have been more direct.

It is over a decade now and so much has happened since that moment in time. Perhaps the clarity only comes after the contracts made between people have occurred. Maybe it is not a map but a music sheet, written and rewritten. Perhaps the genre of the music is known beforehand yet the notes are created one moment at a time. Maybe we all have the power of creation to live the lives we want yet when single notes come together and are played, the effect is amazing.

Maybe it is time to acknowledge that there are conductors of our lives who are gently pulling invisible threads in a concert of improvisation. The signs, the synchronicity, are placed in our awareness. Yet if we know there is choice and personal responsibility, sometimes it may take a while for the music to be heard. When it is, we know that the time and the space was perfect and the music is not ours alone.

Thank You

There are moments in time that stay etched on our hearts forever. I knew the lady had given me a gift, an insight into eternity, that day when she reached out her hand. There are times I return to that moment as if it is still there—a dimension of perfect love. I know with such sincerity that we were not related on earth yet we were soul messengers.

When I accepted the opportunity to write a chapter for this multi-author book with Sunny Dawn Johnston, I could *feel* the lady smiling again. I acknowledged in an instant that she wanted our story shared—the meeting of two strangers who felt the tug on the heart of some invisible thread and the alignment of synchronicities that helped ensure the gift was shared.

ANNIE JARRETT-KEFFELER

After glancing at Sunny Dawn Johnston's Facebook page announcing an eight week online intensive writing course, **_Annie Jarrett-Keffeler_** discovered her niche for writing after signing on for this class in late 2014. She is the author of _Bentley the Big Basset_ series sharing the memories and lessons Annie and her husband, Ryan, experienced from their uniquely lovable basset hound before losing his battle with cancer.

Annie and Ryan live in rural North Dakota on seventeen acres with several animals. Along with her writing, Annie works part time with individuals with disabilities and also owns The Journey Home with AJK where she works with animals and their owners. She, along with her husband, friends, and family are in the process of starting a therapeutic riding program called A Moment of Freedom to help individuals receive the beneficial physical and emotional therapy horses can provide.

ACKNOWLEDGEMENT

For those who had faith in me, especially my husband Ryan, my mom, dad, brothers and the entire Jarrett and Keffeler families; my soul sisters: Ann, Angie, Chelsey, Elisha, and Paula. I want to thank my Anne Carlsen Center family, the supportive ladies of the CR club and Crystal for the "nudge" and always encouraging me. To Connie and Shanda, I will always be eternally grateful. Thank you to Adie for all your help, now and in the future.

DEDICATION

This chapter is dedicated to my grandparents and many other loved ones who have all gone before me and continue to love me and guide me.

Connect with Annie

Email: rakrandr.2349@gmail.com

Social Media

www.facebook.com/TheJourneyHomewithAJK.

www.facebook.com/anniekeffeler

www.facebook.com/anniejarrettkeffeler

CHAPTER THIRTEEN

Take the Hit

By Annie Jarrett-Keffeler

I had been receiving Reiki for around five years and had owned my own business, The Journey Home With AJK. I had taken many classes to learn about the chakras to help me in clearing my own energy, grounding, learning to listen to my little inner Annie, and connecting with my guides and guardian angels. I started finding *me* in this process.

I began to notice positive changes occurring in my daily life. My marriage improved immediately and I started letting go of anger and animosity toward people that I had allowed to make me feel unintelligent, powerless and unloved. I coped better with negative coworkers and a negative environment. My dream of living in the country and owning horses had become a reality and I was connecting and trusting my intuition and gut instincts that I know we are all born with. I experienced wonderful miracles such as hearing my gramma whisper in my ear a few years after she died on my birthday. She whispered, "I love my North Dakota grandbabies and my North Dakota great-grandbabies." I had never felt such pure, unconditional love as I did that very moment. But I still had lessons to learn and to share. Little did I know that what I had learned would help save my life in a matter of a few short minutes and that the two biggest lessons for me were yet to be learned.

Sometime in January of 2013, I started to have a strange reoccurring dream. I thought it was a Reiki client sitting in the driver's seat of a car. Every time this dream occurred, I was in the seat of a car that would slam into the bumper bar with orange reflective tape at the bottom and rear of an enclosed semi-trailer. This reoccurring dream terrified me so much I would bolt into an upright position trembling! The dreams continued and

I would say a prayer for those involved and try to go back to sleep. Nothing seemed to come to fruition with this dream and I would ask myself, "Is there a spiritual message I wasn't getting? What message was I not receiving?"

Several months had passed and I was still receiving those specific visions of a client being slammed into the semi-trailer. I got up every morning after the dream and would send out a prayer asking for safety and protection to whomever it involved and I let it go. My husband, an emergency department nurse, was still in bed recovering from a twelve hour shift the day before. So on this morning I fed and exercised my dogs and headed off to work. In addition to my Reiki business I also work at a residential and school facility that works with individuals with special needs.

I turned onto Highway 281 and headed south. I was approaching the by-pass intersection that connects drivers coming from the west off the interstate onto the highway that I was traveling on running north and south. I kept my eye on the traffic approaching the intersection. I had started to notice, from a distance, that a semi-truck pulling an enclosed trailer was approaching the intersection from the west driving eastbound at an unusually fast speed. I took notice and realized I needed to adjust my speed and I slowed down. The closer I got to the intersection the more aware I became that the truck driver was not slowing down. At this point I immediately slowed down while maintaining control of my vehicle the entire time.

I was certain I would be fine. As I continued to slow down, I came to realize the truck driver had not slowed. I pushed even harder on the brake pedal all while still maintaining control of my little two-door car. The truck driver had completely missed the stop sign and I knew I was in trouble. The semi-truck was quickly cutting off any option of skimming past the front end of the cab in the passing lane. I looked to my right to start negotiating my options and I immediately had a vision of my car going end-over-end. The vision continued as I contemplated veering off to the right of the semi into the ditch. I looked to my left but both southbound lanes were now being crossed by the semi at this point. Panic and fear sunk in.

This was how I was going to die? *REALLY?* This was going to be my life's last memory of being on this earth? I was angry, and I was angry with God!

I grew up on a small grains farm in rural North Dakota so I knew and understood exactly where on me and my car this was going to impact—my neck, face and head. I screamed at God, "*This is how my family is going to remember me?*" I thought of my husband Ryan, my parents, my two older brothers and the faces of all my nieces and nephews, my friends and co-workers. This isn't it...this *can't* be it! I AM NOT DONE YET! I know I have more good things to do!

I looked to my left again and I clearly had a vision and also heard voices telling me that even with the snow in the ditch between the northbound lanes and the southbound lanes there was just not enough snow to stop me. I had far too much momentum and would clear the snow in the ditch and be facing oncoming northbound traffic.

My guardian angels were right. There was oncoming northbound traffic as I could still see past the front end of the semi-truck's cab. I was slamming on my brakes when I heard the words being whispered in my right ear, "*Take the hit, you will be fine. Take the hit, you will be fine. Take the hit!*"

I started to brace myself for impact and I realized I was screaming, "NO! NO! NO!" when in an instant my body relaxed. My arms just softened as did my shoulders, head and neck and I also noticed my head being gently but firmly held in place. I had no control over this and I noticed a strong tingling sensation starting at my clavicle moving up and over my head and down the back of my neck. After hearing those words being whispered in my ear I knew I would either have a quick, clean-cut death or I would walk away untouched.

The noise of the impact has gradually faded since that day but it is hard to completely let go of that sound—the sound of my metal car and the glass of my windshield connecting to the driver's side of the trailer right in front of the rear tires. I can still remember the sound of those tires rubbing on the front right panel of my car as the driver continued to drag me through the intersection. I could also hear the air in the brake lines as I was slamming on my horn begging for the driver to stop! The driver did stop.

"I think I'm still alive" was running through my head. I crawled my way out of the driver's window of my crushed car cab and realized that I was whole, and I was alive. I heard God's voice clearly, telling me, "I chose you! Now, I need you to finish."

The week following the accident was an emotional roller coaster with continuous phone calls from the driver's insurance company asking me to relive those moments over and over again, looking for flaws in my story until my husband, Ryan, had told them, "enough!" Over the next few weeks I started receiving treatments; physical therapy, chiropractic, acupuncture, massage and even counseling.

Although I walked away untouched I was miserable. I could not fathom why I walked away from this. How is this possible? I felt the miracle in this process of surviving but I also felt guilt. I felt guilty to be alive. I knew what God has chosen for me to do but the loneliness I was experiencing was all-consuming. I started to emotionally process what I needed to learn from this experience—worthiness and self-love.

My husband and I, by a twist of fate, ended up with an unusable and demolished car. As it sat in our machine shed I finally mustered up the courage to go and really look at it. It was an absolute miracle I survived this. Looking at the crushed cab and shattered windshield, I gave my gratitude to this car for being strong enough to withstand such an impact. I thanked God for letting me receive this car and for letting it go. I started connecting to my true self. I started really receiving visions and messages from my angels. I started sharing my story about the accident, what I felt, saw, sensed and heard. People didn't shun me for sharing my message from God, either. It was amazing! I reconnected to my long lost best friend. I discovered who my true friends were and I knew what God had chosen for me.

The words *A Moment of Freedom* had popped into my head about six months after my accident. This was to be the name of the equine therapeutic riding program that I, along with my husband, a close friend, and my oldest brother, was to start. My aching and longing to work with horses and individuals with special needs as a child was starting to now make sense. This is what God had intended me to do. This program is a work in progress today, as anything is, but I have never felt as guided as I feel with this. This too will help me heal.

I have continued to be grateful and open to new blessings and opportunities. After losing my beloved nine-year-old basset hound Bentley to cancer, I had received a much needed Reiki session where I was guided to take our memories of Bentley and to write them down as they came to me. "These will be written in children's books someday," shared my friend. In typical Annie fashion I thought, "Huh? Oh, ok." I took note of what my friend was saying during the Reiki session and kind of let it go, but this feeling wouldn't go away. It was very strong. It was the same feeling I had when I knew and felt I was being guided to start the process of the therapeutic riding program.

The next day, Christmas Eve day, I took the advice of buying index cards from my Reiki session and when I felt guided, I started writing down the memories my husband and I had of Bentley. A few days later I noticed Sunny Dawn Johnston had posted an advertisement for an eight week online intensive writing course. The stars aligned and I signed up. I struggled with my lack of worthiness and self-love throughout those eight weeks from several years before and right after my car accident.

Clicking the send button on my rough draft of my Bentley book was an emotional struggle. What if my course instructors Shanda and Connie hated this? What am I doing? I can't do this! What if I never felt good enough? To my amazement both of my instructors loved my Bentley book and I, after thirty-six years, finally started to love myself. I now, to my shock and amazement, have a publisher for my beloved Bentley series!

That accident caused me to really see that I needed to work on self-love and that I *am* worthy. After connecting with Shanda and Connie I felt empowered to start cutting the emotional cord to those who made me feel less than worthy. I started taking my power back in a pure and loving way. For the first time I started to feel really worthy and good about who I am. My accident made me realize I am safe, I am loved, and I am protected.

In my writing I *feel* Safe, Loved and Protected. I am now letting go of my fear of failure and allowing in the feeling of faith. I am being divinely guided with my writing, my RAK Animal Reiki and Rehabilitation business and the wonderful riding program my team and I are building. I love who I am. I am fearless and unashamed and I am proud.

I am safe, I am loved and I am protected—and you are too! I listened to my guardian angels and spirit guides that miraculous day, March 13, 2013. If you add those numbers up (3+1+3+2+0+1+3) they add up to thirteen—I guess it's my lucky number. In fact, I am coming to you from Chapter Thirteen in this book!

Since my accident, I have continued to feel safe, loved and protected. I realize I don't have to count my blessings. *I feel them*!

CHERYL LYNNE

Cheryl Lynne holds a Master's degree in Social Work, is a certified Mind, Body, Spirit Practitioner, Angel Therapy Practitioner, and Reiki Master. She offers spiritual guidance to those facing loss, trauma, and grief from death, divorce, addiction and abuse.

Having triumphed over several insurmountable challenges herself, Cheryl developed the wisdom, courage, and experience as a transformational teacher to help clients move through patterns of stagnation into vibrancy and True-Self living. Along with her intuitive abilities, she utilizes her twenty years of knowledge and training in healing fields such as Emotional Freedom Technique (EFT), energy healing, nutrition, meditation and yoga.

DEDICATION:

To my sweet daughter and friend, Marissa. You tirelessly offer your love and encouragement. To my amazing son, Gavin. You brought me laughter and shared in the fun of spotting angelic traces.

To my devoted sisters, Sandy and Clarin. You're my earth angels who believed in me and sewed grace into the fabric of my life.

To my dear friends Val, Kim, Wendy and Teri with whom sharing steps on this journey is a blessing beyond words.

To Mom. You introduced the world of Spirit to me.

To Aunt Alice and the connection we share.

To Gran.

Connect with Cheryl

Email: cheryllynne444@gmail.com to help transform your life into the life you were born to live!

CHAPTER FOURTEEN

Covered in Wings of Love

By Cheryl Lynne

On threads of serendipity, Spirit sends us messages of love and guidance, masterfully weaving us together in one common and exquisite tapestry. Ironically, while in the moment, we often cannot understand the artful placement of each strand of the people and experiences in our lives. Like examining a piece of woven art too closely, it appears uneven, distorted, unclear or perhaps, disturbing. However, if we are patient and take a step back with trust, we start to see that the swirls and jagged markings within the tapestry actually depict the feathered wings of angels sent to keep us held fast in the Loom of Life and tied to Spirit.

My Grandmother was one of these angelic threads that drew stitches within the embroidery of my life and colored it with comfort. Was it a coincidence that her oldest and youngest daughters got pregnant at the same time and delivered what seemed like twins within a week of each other? I was one of these. When Gran held me for the first time, there was an immediate bond as all the promises we had thread together in spirit began weaving a delicate pattern in our lives.

Gran's home quickly became one my favorite places to visit. She would greet us with a smile on her round face that framed her chocolate-brown eyes, a gentle hug, and a well-stocked cookie cabinet. Sitting on her patio telling jokes and sipping lemonade, were some of my fondest times with Gran. Her laugh was like soda, bubbling up softly and flavoring the air as we sat amused by the darting hummingbirds drawing their own sweet drink from Gran's numerous feeders. She adored these birds especially and had many collectibles of them in her home. Early in childhood I did not realize how my time with Gran would influence my development and relationships in life.

Often, when events line up with such providence, we are unable to deny the divine energy within them that tie us together. On one such occasion, Spirit sent a magical manifestation of this connection while living in the Midwest far from family. During my first pregnancy I sang unabashedly to myself and my unborn baby, several poignant verses of my favorite song, *Amazing Grace,* as I journeyed to work each morning. I often wept as the words and energy of this hymn swirled around us in the car and lit up the space in tandem with the sunrise—making it a spiritual practice that elevated my soul.

One day, just before Christmas, I got a rare package in the mail from Gran. As I unwrapped the gift and realized what I was holding, my mouth fell open and tears flooded my eyes. She sent me a small blanket with the print of sheet music and curly words spelling out the lyrics to *Amazing Grace.* I never told *anyone* about my sacred, singing practice! Of all the gifts she could have sent, or all the prints to have chosen, Gran selected this woven cover with its thick threads writing the beautiful message I had been singing for months! I called her immediately to thank her, but the words tumbled out clumsily. She did not need clear words; we both understood why she felt impressed to send it. I wrapped the blanket around my shoulders and absorbed her embrace through the distance. This was but one of many synchronistic events that occurred with Gran.

On a different occasion, while away on a retreat with my sister, I was given another most precious gift. My sister and I were on a much deserved break from work and motherhood and had pulled up to Gran's house to spend our last night there before returning home. It was the first time we would stay with her since Grandpa died and we were eager to see how she was coping. However, that enthusiasm was pushed aside soon after we parked. A phone call came through from my husband that quickly moved from bewildering to heart-breaking and left me sobbing and fearful. Seeing that the conversation was very difficult for me, my sister left the car to give me privacy. When I ended the call, I cleaned up my face, inhaled self-encouragement, and with a pressed-on smile crossed Gran's threshold. Seconds after I entered, her short frame padded around the corner to greet me. I moved in to hug her, but the moment she enclosed me in her arms, my throat caught and I began to weep all over again. The bolstering I had meant to offer to her in her bereavement morphed into the comforting embrace I so desperately needed for myself. The contents of that phone call, with all of its painful patterns that continued to tear at my marriage, toppled over me. I tried to get my voice to apologize for this silly reception, but my tears flowed unceasingly. Gran knew what my soul needed. She gently held my head on her shoulder and spoke softly to me. Even though I towered over her small stature, she felt bigger than me and I was transported back to being a child. I relaxed and sunk deep into her safe and careful hold, wrapped in the wings of an angel. As time waited, draped around us, Gran slowly and almost unperceptively lifted the weight from my burdened heart and bore it on her own worn and rounded shoulders. Peace was carried in the vibration of her voice assuring me, and perhaps herself, that everything would be alright. She did not press me for information or ask what she could do. She just stood with me, present and still, weaving a powerful message into my spirit.

This moment in infinity could not have been laced together more seamlessly. However small and simple, it became one of the most profound markers in my life. I was imbued with a complete feeling of safety, security and utter acceptance. I pull it from my memory pocket in dark times to stitch myself back together and remind myself that I am loved and supported.

A short time later Gran became ill and went into the hospital. Sadly, she had just endured the news of her sister's death and would now miss her funeral. I sat with her for a few hours and chatted, hoping to offer comfort, then promised to return with details of her sister's memorial. After a couple of days, I stepped into her room wearing a smile of cheer, only to be halted by drawn faces sunk in the dense energy of sadness. Gran was rapidly slipping into increasing frailty. How was this possible? I just saw her and we had talked and laughed together. This seemed illusory. We spoke with doctors and nurses trying to uncover a solution, but she had moved beyond their ability to pull her back into wellness. *No Gran! I can't lose you,* I sorrowed. I couldn't get my heart to catch up to the reality before me.

I wanted to halt the loom and stop all the pedals from weaving this part of my life! Viewing it so closely, it was dismal and disheartening. I tried to remember all the last things I had said to her...or what she had said to me! Did I really hear her? Or did I cover over the fear with jovial remarks? All of these thoughts whirled around with the beeping monitors and nurses bustling in and out past family. I wondered if Gran knew how much her presence in my life meant to me. Did *I* even know?

No one was prepared. We envisioned Gran waddling back into her 85-year-old self with canvas shoes and curly hair, smiling her reassurance through those delicious eyes. I watched my mother and aunt, the dynamic duo with twin pregnancies so long ago, now encased in glass, carefully navigating the confusing barrage of choices and hospital protocol. These two brave daughters bore the burden of the choices that had to be made and forced themselves to speak the words that felt impossible to say. If she was to be kept alive by the machines, she would have to stay at our mercy. Was she telling us she was prepared to go? I wondered if Gran's timing had been carefully woven as a twin transition with her sister, a line of connection with the paired births from decades before. Had we been gathered to celebrate *their* new births? With shallow breath, we listened while the nurses spoke of what they could do to help ease her passing.

Even though she had faded into a coma, I could feel that Gran was peaceful with the decision to go. I sat at her left, her heart side—the part of her that carried so much burden in her life and was now the part that was taking her to the other side. I pressed my cheek to hers and wept as my throat struggled to push out my last words. Overwhelmed with what I could possibly say to capture a lifetime of feelings and squeeze them into one moment, my heart formed the words, "I love you Gran. You lent me so much strength and taught me of love." To my great astonishment, I heard three delicate sounds pulse from her like a faint heartbeat, "I... love... you." My head sprung upright and I scanned her face expecting to see her open eyes in a gentle smile, but she was still. My eyes darted to my mother who sat at Gran's other side and we both marveled at the great miracle we had just witnessed. Gran's spirit pierced through all physical limitations to sew that final message into the fabric of this moment!

Our family held each other as we surrounded her bed and sang. Gran gracefully moved into her new life. My sadness was replaced with sacredness as I absorbed the amazing privilege it was to witness this holy transition. I envisioned the joy she would feel reuniting with her loved ones, and smiled as her beautiful energy filled the room and passed through us.

In preparation for the funeral, I asked my mother if I could offer the song that connected me so tenderly to Gran all those years ago. I had not sung a solo in public before, and certainly never a cappella! I stood nervously before the crowd and closed my eyes. I pictured Gran in front of me with her smooth face wearing an approving smile under those delectable eyes, and I lifted my voice. The lyrics flowed from my heart and passed through my lips as *Amazing Grace* filled the air and knit us through time.

For a long while, I could hardly bear the quiet emptiness that Gran used to fill. No more hugs as only she could give, no more looking into her coffee eyes, or enjoying porch chats with hummingbird entertainment. I yearned to sense her near me again. I gently called to Gran, envisioning her sweet eyes and feeling her hands on my face. As I turned my gaze, there it was hovering near. It did a loop in the air and darted in a dancing flight pattern. The iridescent hues of a most exquisite hummingbird lit up before me! A burst of laughter escaped my lips and tears wet my eyes. *Gran, is that you?* Back came the little creature—this time just a fly by. My breath paused in wonder. Had Gran appeared within the energy of this wee bird, like the ones we had spent adoring together ages ago? Yes. "Thank you. I love you." I whispered, hand over my heart.

I encountered many of these lovingly designed instances where I was given support and encouragement. One of the most important of these came at a time when my widely predictable future was shred before me and wrenched from my hands. After more than twenty years, I was facing the harrowing reality that my marriage was ending. My heart was ripped in two and the shock of it was crippling. I now realize my spirit chose this man to help me progress and sew into my life the strands of forgiveness, compassion, self-love and nurturing. Yet, in that moment of despair, grief and agony, I felt like a lose thread torn from its cloth, dangling weak and vulnerable, unable to find purchase. I questioned whether I had the strength to endure one more moment.

I drove to find solace in a yoga class, but could not stop the torrent of tears that had been unleashed. Feeling defeated, I pulled my car to a private spot, and climbed out. Needing to move through the overwhelming sorrow, I paced in agony—agony I felt from the loss, betrayal, anger and heartache that seared inside me. I implored Spirit to give me strength. I had nothing left to keep me standing and could not see enough light to guide me through.

Exhausted, I slipped back into my car and pulled the door closed. I dragged in just one stifled breath, when up to my window fluttered a black and white tuxedo-adorned messenger! I stopped my breath from clouding the glass and riveted my eyes on this tiny guardian. A small hummingbird with great energy hovered four inches from my face, as though bouncing on a tightrope. We held each other's gaze for several seconds which seemed like a looking glass into eternity. I couldn't help but chuckle while new tears ran stripes down my cheeks.

An invisible line of love darned the frayed edges of my heart as this miniature manifestation zipped and zapped outside my window. It returned twice to check on me after pulling sustenance from nearby flowers then flitted away. I felt the same release inside my body as the time in Gran's entry when she stepped under the weight of my burden. This precious instant expressed the comfort I longed for, not only from Gran, but from Spirit and the angelic realm, all letting me know I was not alone. I was loved and watched over, entwined eternally.

Undeniably, the Universe endeavors to keep souls stitched together. Like the wonder of Gran's blanket, specific events are too carefully woven to be happenstance. Many people in our lives bring with them healing fibers to help us patch the holes in the textile of our human experience torn by others as well as ourselves. During her life, Gran artfully mended tears I didn't realize I had and the energy of her heart continues to touch my life in the winged manifestations of love that arrive uniquely timed. As I look back on the many magical moments strung together, I see they bear the beautiful Tapestry of Life tenderly securing us all to Spirit with everlasting cords. I am so grateful for this Amazing Grace.

VERNITA SOLTIS

Vernita Soltis is an Intuitive Life Coach, Mind-Body-Spirit Practitioner, Certified Ordained Minister and Angel Instructor Practitioner in the Phoenix, Arizona area. As a military spouse for twenty-one years, she knew the challenges of long separations and raising three kids on her own even prior to the tragic loss of her husband in a dirt bike accident in 2013. These life experiences brought a shift in her spiritual path, turning her focus toward helping women and men come to terms with grief, loss and unexpected life change and achieve personal empowerment along the way.

Vernita works with others who are struggling with grief and terminal illnesses, depression and social anxiety. She also works with those struggling with the feeling that they have lost their passion for life and who wants to move toward living their life purpose.

DEDICATION

I dedicate my chapter to my late husband, Ret. Navy SEAL CPO Bruce C. Soltis, who was my greatest teacher, soulmate, lover and friend. To my mother Shirley A. Solomon, we were destined to help each other in this life and we will continue to always do so. To my children Briana L. Soltis, Tyler L. Soltis, and Mariah J. Soltis, my little mini me. Thank you for the gift of your love, hope and grace to move on with my new normal.

Connect with Vernita

Email: vernita@vernitasoltis.com

Website: www.vernitaevesoltis.com

Social Media: www.facebook.com/vernita.soltis

CHAPTER FIFTEEN

Moving Through Grief
With Grace and Ease

By Vernita Soltis

Before I met my husband, I was a struggling eighteen-year-old trying to make it in the world alone. My parents divorced when I was three and I had been on my own since the age of seventeen. My home life was toxic with a drug and alcohol addicted single mother who was hooked on heroin most of my early teens. To make matters worse, I had also been sexually abused by a family member.

My father was not in the picture much of my young life except when I was sent to live with him for a year in my early teens. My mother could not handle a teenager due to her drug addiction and raising a child on her own with no support from my father was too much for her. I have never blamed her for I know she only did what she knew to do at the time. My mother and I have since come to a very close and loving relationship nurtured with her sobriety of thirty years. We have both spoken in great depth about how we were brought together into this lifetime to help and teach each other the lessons for which we contracted. This was our life plan.

I volunteered for this path; actually we both did. I came forth to help her move through her addictions and it was so profound that it amazes me to this day. We are soul connected, just as soulmates. You do not need to be a lover to be a soulmate for soulmates come in many forms and relationships through your human life from your past lives to the present. We are all connected long before this life.

I was told from a young age that I was special and that I had a rare gift of intuition. Being an only child, I didn't fit in with my peers, and struggling with dyslexia only served to make matters worse. I have always had a knowing of things that I could not fully explain. I could not relate to it at the time, but I seemed to know things intuitively, even as a child. These gifts have gotten stronger as I got older—especially after my husband suddenly passed away in 2013 in a dirt bike accident at the age of fifty-two.

I met my husband, Bruce C. Soltis, thirty years ago when he was a veteran Navy SEAL of twenty-one years. At the time he was at BUDS (Basic Underwater Demolition School) in the Special Forces in the Navy. As a student he had been held back due to breaking his neck during a training exercise in a prior BUDS class. I was aware of who he was through mutual friends in our small town of Coronado, California. We had never really spoken or noticed each other until the night we met at an after-hours party. I didn't recognize him at first because when I had seen him around town before his head was in a halo brace from his neck injury and his head was shaved due to having been in training.

At the time, I was coming out of a heart-break following a breakup with a man I was going to marry six months prior so I was certainly not looking for a relationship. Bruce arrived at my friend's home with some buddies, but this time he had longer hair and no halo brace. We stayed up all night talking and I knew there was a mutual attraction. When the night was over he asked for my phone number. There were no cell phones back then, and at this time in my life, being the smart-ass girl I was, and with a large chip on my shoulder, I looked at him and said, "Why? You're not going to call!" He told me in the years since that he was thinking to himself, "Why that little shit! I'm going to prove her wrong." This has always made me smile plus it gave him something to prove.

I realized that I had left my wallet at my girlfriend's house and unbeknownst to me Bruce had volunteered to bring it to me so she gave him my home address. My home was twenty-five minutes out of his way back to the barracks on base. But the doorbell rang and there he was…with my wallet in his hands, smiling at me with that treasure cat smile and twinkle in his eyes. I will always remember that about him.

He spent the rest of the weekend with me and it sealed the deal on a four-year courtship and finally, marriage. We lived in many places, both state side and overseas and had three beautiful children together.

All three of my children have been my rock. I was grateful that they were adults and not little children when they lost their father. It was on the morning of September 5, 2013 when Bruce went for that fateful dirt bike ride at the age of fifty-two. His decomposing body wasn't discovered in the Arizona desert until the morning of September 6. Temperatures in the desert had soared to 111 degrees during the search and rescue.

I could not feel closure with his death. We were all in shock. All I could think was that we are talking about a NAVY SEAL here. Bruce knew how to survive in all types of terrain. In fact, just the year before he was riding in the same area on his dirt bike and crashed resulting in four broken ribs, as we learned later in the week. Despite his injuries, he still pulled the bike out on his own. He was tough and strong and we always considered him invincible. Looking back, I remember saying, "No, not my Bruce. He isn't dead; he just broke an arm or a leg and he is waiting for help to arrive. He knows to wait for help if unable to get out of a situation."

The investigator told us that Bruce had done everything right; he had his cell phone on, he had his wallet and a gallon of water on hand and was fully geared up from head to toe. This tragedy had our entire community in shock. Bruce was one of those men that you either loved him or hated him, but if you hated him you ended up loving him in the end. He was personable and witty, charismatic, extremely intelligent and very spiritual with his God.

I remember standing up after the funeral service and turning around in the church; it was standing room only all the way out of the church. It was surreal. What an honor to have known him and loved him as long as I had.

Bruce was selfless. We drove the kids down to Baja Mexico for spring break one year when they were small. That week Bruce ended up saving the lives of three people: one from a fire, another from drowning in the hotel pool, and he saved a baby that was choking on food in the restaurant. He was the type of man that would go to the grocery to pick up items for me and come back with flowers. He needed no excuse or a holiday to surprise me with flowers. Bruce knew how to live life with no regrets and he always tested the limits.

Losing my husband so suddenly was a life-changing event that catapulted me into tremendous personal and spiritual growth. It set me on the path to finding my inner self and purpose. Who am I? What am I doing here? I still struggle to find the answers but I also know it is a process. After all, we all have to walk our own path. Who among us doesn't?

I know my husband and I were soulmates and had lived many lives with each other, as well as with our children. I know it was our life contract; I know the love never ends and is everlasting, yet at first I was very angry when he passed.

I went into automatic survival mode, my autopilot switched on. The years of being a military wife had taught me that I was expected to hold down the fort and not to ask questions. I went through the motions and did what Bruce and I discussed when he was alive. He told me what I was supposed to do and who I was supposed see if anything happened to him. He wanted to make sure my life did not crash financially. It was almost as if he knew he was going to die at a young age. He wanted me to be taken care of.

We would have long talks that would last well into the night. Bruce shared that he was ready spiritually if he was to die tomorrow, and that he had no regrets. He would say that he did not want to leave us but he knew he was ready if it happened. The very week prior to the accident, I had the thought flash through my head, *what would I do if he dies? How would I live? How would I survive?*

I believe I intuitively knew the accident was going to happen and I blamed myself because I didn't know if I could have stopped him from going out on the dirt bike that morning. But I must realize, no, I was at work, and when stubborn Bruce wanted to do something he was going to do it. I believe that is why our marriage lasted thirty years. He would never give up on most anything, or us, when I could have easily done so coming from a divorced family.

I have had many teachers along my life's path—good and bad, too many to count. Yes, even my abusive biker father and a family member that sexually abused me at the age of five. I learned to let go and forbid the past to hold me hostage. I don't hold animosity or hatred for my father. He was a hard ass, and not a very nice person in general with a bad temper,

Moving Through Grief with Grace and Ease | Vernita Soltis

but I knew he loved me. He made me tough and strong so I could deal with life and not take shit from others. After dying from cancer twelve years ago, I found closure with visits from my father in dreams that were very real. I had a similar experience when my grandfather passed. We had unfinished business. I have been told this happens when you have a 'heart connection' with the ones you love that have passed.

I know my father still watches over me when I'm riding my motorcycle as well as my husband. Bruce and I rode together on separate Harleys. He would look over at me when we rode and say, "That's my girl."

Though a part of me knows that Bruce left us doing what he loved, I cannot be angry with that. Yes, I am sad and I miss his physical form, but I *feel* his presence with me all the time. He visits my dreams, less now than at first, but when I am struggling with life or feeling down, he pops in and has a chat with me. He knows—I've got this.

Four months after Bruce passed away I was urged by a friend to go see a well-known physic medium. She said maybe I could get help to gain closure with his passing and maybe get some questions answered, too. So, I visited the physic medium. She shared that Bruce was sending me someone. Stunned, I thought, "Okay…what does this mean, or is she just full of it?" She added that when our paths crossed it would be so significant that I would know him because he would have the same name or same birthday, something would be the same. Would I meet someone by the name of Bruce or have his same birth date? She said it would be soon, but what does that mean? I put this out of my head and went on with life, not really sure where I was going.

As the months turned and May was upon us, I decided to return to the physic medium for guidance for my son. I knew she had similar issues with her son as I was having with mine at the time. Again she says that Bruce was sending me someone and that he knew what type of man I needed in my life. She said it would be very soon.

June came and I was at a bike rally where I met a man. We chatted about rides coming up and ended up exchanging emails which turned into lengthy phone calls. We spoke for four hours on the phone. I never do this nor did he as neither of us like talking on the phone. In conversation I asked him when his birthday was. He replied May twenty-first. I got goose bumps immediately. That is *my* birthday! I went to sleep that night and just before waking, I heard a voice saying that his name is the same name as Bruce's father who had died in a plane crash when he was seventeen years old.

We had an instant connection and we fell hard for each other, but we also got scared and felt it was going too fast, too soon. We took a break for three months, but he came back into my life just before the holidays and spent time with us through New Year's. My kids loved him as he is a wonderful man. We continued to struggle with unfinished business on his end that he needed to work out. It had nothing to do with me, and I eventually acknowledged that I was not able to help him with his demons.

He did so much for me, though. He helped me reduce Bruce's military items from three storage units down to one and helped me sell much of it, never wanting any payment for it. My late husband was a pack rat and kept everything. You can imagine thirty years of *stuff*!

My friend and I are not together as a couple now. But I know we will always be friends and I believe the reason he came into my life (or Bruce sent him to me) was to show me that I really could love again. I was grateful for his help in clearing out the past for it was a huge undertaking.

Relationships don't always work out romantically. Perhaps the time isn't right, but they are placed in our lives to help us learn to see the bigger picture. It is that invisible thread for which I am forever grateful. Threads have woven themselves in my life to help mold and take me along the path, never knowing where I am going to land.

Of course there is never a perfect time for death, but this was the contract and everyone was in place to be able to handle it in the best way they could at the time. Our children took his death better than most, if there is ever such a concept. This is what I call moving through grief with grace and ease. It is the strong sense of knowing that this was going to happen and how we would need to play it out for our continued wellbeing.

I know my family of five has lived many lives together, interchanging our modalities in each life as we are presented them. We are old souls together—as a spirit family—connected forever by the invisible thread.

GIULIANA MELO

Giuliana Melo is passionate about non-traditional healing methods and working with angels. Her own experience of walking through and healing from cancer caused an awakening in her spirit when she was asking _why me_? Then she realized _why not me_? and experienced true grace in the process. She recently retired from a thirty-one-year career in healthcare and has become a certified Mind, Body, and Spirit Practitioner. She has been married for twenty-eight years and has a seventeen-year-old son.

Giuliana has incredibly strong faith and encourages many through her coaching practice. She provides intuitive angel card readings and Reiki. She is an author contributor to the bestselling book _365 Days of Angel Prayers_ in addition to _The Book of Love_. She is a Kindness Ambassador having created the Kindness Crew Calgary Society which is committed to providing a hand-up to the homeless and performing random acts of kindness and sits on the advisory board of the DreamSTRONG™ Foundation.

ACKNOWLEDGEMENT

I am blessed to know Sunny Dawn Johnston, Connie Gorrell and Shanda Trofe. Their unending love and support has been a lifeline that I appreciate more than words can say. Thank you, ladies.

DEDICATION

This chapter is dedicated to my strong Faith and Love of God and to the friends and family that He has provided to help get me through this amazingly beautiful life. I would like to thank my mom, Mary Giuliano, who means the world to me. I also thank my husband Paulo Melo and my dear son Paulo, Jr. for all their unending love and support.

Connect with Giuliana

Email: jmelo10@shaw.ca

Website: www.giulianamelo.com

Social Media

www.facebook.com/julie.g.melo
www.facebook.com/HealWithGiuliana/

www.twitter.com/Jmelo10Julie

CHAPTER SIXTEEN

The Invisible Healing Threads

By Giuliana Melo

When God laid out the plan for your life, He lined up the right people, the right breaks, and the right opportunities. He has blessings that have your name on them. If you stay in faith, at the right time you will come into what already belongs to you. It is a prepared blessing. —Joel Osteen

It is an invisible thread that bonds us to the precise people, breaks, opportunities and blessings meant for us. We are all connected. Indiscernible threads tie humans together regardless of distance and death. The connection is love. Love is what we are. Love is where we come from and where we return. Love unites us by that invisible thread that cannot be seen but can be recognized.

Weak threads connect us to people we meet in a class or event. Strong, silky threads are those that connect family and friends. These threads are so durable that you can go days, months or even years without contact, or conversation, yet always knows that they are there for you. Coarse threads link persons who are there to teach lessons. They may cause wounds. Through those wounds, the parts of ourselves that require healing are brought to light. We may bleed but the silky threads help us to heal with all the love that is available to us. It is true—an invisible thread connects all of us who are destined to meet, regardless of time, place and circumstance. The thread may stretch or tangle but it never breaks. It may feel snapped because of pain inflicted on the heart.

It is my hope that you will open your heart to each type of thread that enters your life. Both the silky golden and the dull coarse strands are much like a spider as she weaves her gossamer web. I hope that you will find a way to weave these threads into a brilliant, beautiful life.

The creator of our invisible thread is GOD. God places individuals into our lives so we can learn, grow, heal and expand in love. We never meet by accident; everyone we encounter is sent to teach us something. There is value and beauty in every thread representing a personal connection.

Examples of golden threads are those in marriage and family—the tie to siblings, children, parents, grandparents, ancestors, aunts, uncles, cousins. There are the ties to your nationality; friend ties all over the world. The healing, invisible thread in my life is one I wove with the help of God, the angels and my team in the physical world—doctors, nurses, and health care providers.

The invisible faith thread leads us straight to our Creator to whom I prayed for guidance. I learned to trust my intuition. It has led me in the right direction and I always ask God for the next right step. He illuminates the next thread in an invisible array of color, which is the essence of the Archangels. They have helped me in ways that are miraculous. God provides these messengers of light for all. We ask for help. We allow that help into our lives. I believe with all my heart that they will help when I open myself to receive their amazing assistance, guidance, love and support.

Though you cannot see or feel this multi-stranded invisible thread, it exists. Those who are meant to stay or return to you are tied to you. Death in the physical sense does not break that strong tie. I thank God for each of my threads. I am grateful for the ties that bind us together for I know we are never alone. How amazing is that? It is amazing *grace*. By the grace of God and with his invisible thread I am healing. Through the synchronicity of life, which are meaningful coincidences, He leads us to the right people, breaks, opportunities, and blessings.

With everything that has happened to you, you can either feel sorry for yourself, or treat what has happened as a gift. Everything is either an opportunity to grow, or an obstacle to keep you from growing. You get to choose.

—Wayne Dyer

When I was diagnosed with stage-three peritoneal cancer I felt as though I was going to die. I was paralyzed with fear. I could not work or think straight. I prepared for the worst. I showed my husband where the life insurance documents and wills were. I was living, but barely. I couldn't wait for the surgery. Luckily, when my gynecologist delivered the diagnosis, my sister and husband were with me. My sister worked for a cancer clinic and had connections. She expedited the process and I saw the oncologist right away—surgery was scheduled within the month!

The day of surgery I awakened with a sense of urgency and with a lot of trust and faith that the surgeon would remove all the cancer. I wanted my body clean and clear so I asked God for help and to bless the doctors and nurses. I asked to be taken care of by Him.

It took several hours after the surgery to recover from the anesthesia. When I awoke, it was to unbelievable pain. While still groggy, I was returned to my room where my husband and parents were anxiously waiting. That first day was a blur of pain and family members leaning over me asking repeatedly how I was feeling. I responded that I was okay and I believed it, because I instinctively began to visualize the area of my peritoneum and pelvis clean and clear of all cancer cells. I kept imagining a white light running inside me. At that moment I started to love myself and I knew I had to change my life. With that realization, peace enveloped me. My inner fears dissipated and I believe I experienced what receiving the true grace of God feels like, and I started to understand what it meant. I changed the negative thoughts of pity and of asking God *why me*? I instead asked, why *not* me? God takes care of his children, and God would take care of me. Suddenly my invisible threads became visible.

My family nurtured me back to health. They cradled me in love like a newborn baby. My beautiful mom came for a month each time I had surgery. I had two major abdominal surgeries. She became my nurse, psychiatrist, mentor, teacher, shopper, cleaner, caregiver, prayer warrior and so much more; but most of all she was there as my mom and I was her baby. And regardless of age, when in need, we all crave the physical and emotional arms of our mothers.

My sister who has gone through her own battle with poor health brought her knowledge to bear in my care, and became my greatest cheerleader and best friend. She was at my side when I needed her. My dad, who is sensitive and quiet, kept his feelings and emotions inside, seemingly never knowing what to say to me; yet, mom told me that for him, the thought of losing his first child overwhelmed him. For him, regardless of age, I will always be one of his two baby girls. My brother Nick is rough on the outside but gentle inside. He came and sat with me, not wanting to believe that I had been diagnosed with cancer, but always supportive and ready to listen with loving kindness. He was willing to help with my son, to take him out and keep him occupied, and as a sibling, he is the one most like me. My brother Peter, who is the youngest, and has a psychology degree from the University of Guelph, became my psychologist and voice of reason. He was and is a great counsellor and someone I turn to very often. Perhaps what also accelerated my recovery was my extended family of aunts, uncles, and cousins, who are an amazing support team.

The empathy of family and friends who brought food, magazines, toiletries, flowers, books, and cards was also a path to healing. The visits were an incredible gift. Each time someone came the conversation encouraged and empowered me to want to keep getting better. Next to the golden thread of God, this thread has been and remains my lifeline. I don't take this thread for granted. It is strong and unbreakable.

The thread that surprised and blessed me the most and made me feel safest was the one to my husband Paulo. He talks tough, is very confident and works incessantly. He has been an excellent provider during our twenty-eight years of marriage. He does not suffer health problems and even if exhausted from overwork seems to have an abundance of energy. He comes from a family that has no understanding of what it means to lack confidence, either. Little did I know at that inauspicious start of this health journey what a magnitude of blessing God had given me when I met Paulo. This thread has been tested, but it has held together. Terrified at the thought of losing me, Paulo held my hand, nurtured my mind and body and brought me back to health. I saw another side to my husband as he began to spend more time taking care of me. He realized that my chemo-riddled body required his healing touch. My greatest gift was meeting Paulo's soul during that time of my recovery. I realize now he was just as vulnerable as I was but he never complained. He took on other duties in addition to his main job. As my mother lived over two hundred miles away and worked after she returned home, he became my doctor and nurse, tending to my wounds. He cleaned, cooked, shopped. He did whatever was necessary. He was present and held my hand during all six chemo sessions; he embraced me when I cried and laughed with me in moments of happiness. I am so blessed by this amazing thread I call my husband's love.

In addition to my own health problems, my twelve-year-old son manifested epilepsy. He just couldn't accept his mommy being sick, bald and not herself. He was hurt by my constant inability to do anything but lie on the sofa. He did not understand how his mom could become a listless person who was unable to go out and participate in all of the activities that we used to do. Most of all he was terrified that he was going to lose me. His body and soul could not take it. I will never forget travelling with Paulo in the car going home from a doctor's visit when I suddenly heard a strange sound and looked back to see that my son had turned blue, choking. We rushed to the hospital emergency room where he was diagnosed with epilepsy. His life was spared that day but the episodes continued. His thread was stretched too thin and at that point so was mine. We had to rely on our faith. We had to trust that God had a plan for all of us to learn and to grow in this experience we call life. Through all of the adversity, God blessed our family. Make-A-Wish Southern Alberta granted a wish for my son to go to Euro-Disney in Paris, and that proved to be the trip of a lifetime for us.

Recognizing all the many blessings while enduring the medical intervention stimulated my spirit. I felt so very connected to everyone. I felt guided by the Holy Spirit. I listened to Hay House Radio where I was introduced to spiritual teachers and wisdoms. I made two trips to Toronto with my mother to see Oprah and the healer, John of God. I went through a spiritual surgery and I could *feel* my healing. I had to trust the process of life and the will of God. I could not live in fear of cancer. I believe that the cancer came as a lesson.

I have made changes in how I react to life. I have made changes to the foods I eat and changed the work I do. I have moved on from my thirty-one-year career in healthcare. I had an invisible thread to the angels and to a life that became illuminated. I share what I have learned with those whom God sends to me.

While writing this I asked the angels if there was a message they wanted me to write. This is what I received:

> *"Every day we wake we are to realize it is a blessing. We are to be grateful and choose to be happy. We can connect the threads. We can ask for help. It is safe to believe and know that there is a power greater than us—that it exists and ties us all together and that this is the thread of LOVE."*

My command is this: Love each other as I have loved you.

—John 15:12

Synchronicity is an amazing occurrence of magic, mystery and miracles. When you experience it once it unlocks your soul to the freedom to experience it daily. Humans tend to think of themselves only as physical beings and forget we are spiritual beings connected to Source. That is the main thread. We have a team of high-vibrational beings helping us on our earth journeys. When we open ourselves to their help they send us signs. Synchronistic events are signs to give us hope, guide us, and help us feel supported. They also help us make decisions. Synchronistic events are magical. I work with angels; I have since I was a little girl. I always knew I had at least one guardian angel. After getting married and purchasing my first home, I felt guided to ask the angels for their names. I was given Nicole, Samantha and Bernadette. That was my guardian angel invisible thread. I was open to receive their names and intuitively believed the information they put into my head and my heart. Later in my life when I was walking through a cancer diagnosis, and healing my physical body due to the chemo and surgeries to rid my body of disease, I was aware of their presence in my life. That was an invisible thread to Heaven. I had help from family in spirit too.

To occupy my mind during the healing process, I went online daily. It provided an invisible thread to family and friends all over the world.

During this time, I discovered the Celebrate Your Life events conference live-streams so I could watch from home. The teacher I felt most connected to was Sunny Dawn Johnston. I joined her mentoring groups, went to her retreats, took her courses and through that invisible thread, I became part of this book. Thank you God, for loving us enough to tie us together with the golden threads of Light.

I am in gratitude to *all* the threads of my life.

JACQUELINE LAMICA

Jacqueline Lamica is a freelance writer who began her career writing poetry and short stories for no one to ever see. She mainly wrote journal entries to vent feelings of happiness and her life experiences and until recently her work had not been published. That changed with an entry titled *Illuminations of the Soul* in a poetry contest sponsored by The Spiritual Writers Network. She is passionate about helping others in need of understanding life's struggles. Currently she is working as a fulltime caregiver for her mother who is fighting the dreadful effects of Alzheimer's disease.

Jacquie is taking steps to further advance her knowledge in aiding the elderly with Alzheimer's and their families. You are invited to read Jacquie's blog where she shares her experiences in this field while documenting her mother's progress and reach out to her if you are guided.

ACKNOWLEDGEMENT

I want to thank Connie Gorrell for seeing in me something that was hidden and pushing me to accept and release the stories and poetry inside of me. I want to thank my daughters for helping me see my way through this commitment to continued care.

DEDICATION

This chapter on *Grace* is dedicated to my beautiful little momma, Margie.

Connect with Jacquie

Email: hddreamin@gmail.com

Website: www.anovicecaregiverblog.com

CHAPTER SEVENTEEN

The Threads of Grace

By Jacqueline Lamica

What is grace? Is it in the way a ballerina moves across her stage with long beautiful legs reaching for the perfect pirouette? Or is it in the peacefulness of a white swan floating on a glassy lake, arching her neck as if to form the outline of a heart? Can grace be seen through a new mother's eyes looking at her newborn child, feeling the absolute glow of love, trust and innocence all wrapped up one beautiful being? Look around you. Grace is ever-changing; never the same except for the fact that it touches each of us in different ways. And such goes gratitude as well.

I have always been one to be grateful for the blessings in my life, but nothing really prepared me for what was to come. I had to relearn the meaning of gratitude and how it presents itself in my daily life. My dear mother was diagnosed with dementia a few years ago. I took on the full-time responsibility of being her primary caregiver as there was no one else available to assist me. My father and mother were married happily for fifty years until he lost his eighteen-year battle with cancer. He did not know that his wife, my mother, would be afflicted with Alzheimer's disease when he asked me to take care of her right before he passed away.

In the beginning it was easy. She had raised me right and I was happy to have this time with her. Since then, her disease has become more challenging and has escalated into Alzheimer's. She now lives with me and it is very difficult watching her become so completely disoriented. Once a brilliant, compassionate person she spends her days and nights struggling to formulate her thoughts, looking around herself at the surroundings as if she has never seen them before. She no longer recognizes everyday things we take for granted every single minute of every single day. At times I feel as though time is spinning around like a Ferris wheel that never stops. It has led me to the next chapter in my journey—learning what grace and gratitude really mean to me and how they show up in my life. Digging deeper into my soul to in search of the true meaning of life is an everyday challenge.

How do beautiful souls arrive at the threshold of grace? Is it through the power of prayer? My mother always had a connection to prayer. Perhaps it is through children taught to respect others and treat them as we would want to be treated. Whatever the reason, I am deeply connected to my mother and strive to do the right thing by her, every moment of the day.

As I grew up there was always someone there for me. I certainly did not grow up on the privileged side of town but I believed with all my heart that all I needed was family and friends by my side. I thought if I tried to do my best and was honest that all would be well in my world. It was a rude awakening when that idea came to a screeching halt, along with what I thought was fair and good in my world! I have witnessed people using others to reach for higher places and what truth and lies can do. I was naïve in the real world. Without my family surrounding me, I discovered a new life where choices had serious consequences. I was blindsided by choices I had made and people I had trusted. I tried to fix what was going wrong but I had no power—or shall I say I gave my power away to someone who had an agenda of their own. Yet, I put my heart and soul into my choice, after all, I had committed myself to doing this. I turned inward, searching deep inside myself to understand why bad things were happening to me. I had never been mean or spoken words that would hurt others. I was the person who tried to uplift and help people. Why was everything going wrong? I learned to be strong and realized this was not my shortcoming but a new lesson I must learn. I survived demeaning words and anger. I didn't want to talk to anyone about these problems because I figured I could solve them myself if I only dug deeper. I had grown up seeing my mother pray. Her beliefs in God helped her rise above any given earthly situation and, like her, that journey has brought me here today.

I learned the art of listening; not just the words that people speak, but listening beyond what their hearts are actually saying, studying their body language, trying to focus on the hurt they carry and reaching out to help uplift them. Where there was darkness, I would shed light. As I practiced this I became very adept at this special talent. I listened carefully and helped anyone that reached out to me and became increasingly more grateful for every experience I had. I knew my life had been blessed because I certainly did not have it as bad as some of the people I was trying to help. This helped me to look at each of my mother's random thoughts and see the struggle she was having, trying to navigate her new life situation.

I began to write poetry to express the feelings I could not understand and found that I would feel better almost immediately. The oppression of hurt lessened and my heart began to feel light and right with every sentence I wrote. The rhyme in the words was easy. I felt enlightened by my own words. Poetry was a gift and it brought me great joy. Poetry helped me to once again feel grateful for what the Spirit had given me.

As time passed I began to give my attention to the great medicine chiefs and how they received uncanny messages from the Spirits above. They are portrayed as calm and all-knowing and I thought *how beautiful* as people are always grateful for wisdom. Wouldn't it be great to understand more of what you cannot see but always knew was there? I believe in angels and knew they must have been with me all along. I don't know how I could I have made it through the years of anger and aggression that surrounded my marriage otherwise. Lady Luck had not protected me and it was not by chance that things happened as they did. I knew there were lessons there for me to learn. This was a life-changing revelation!

Poetry in itself is an act of explanation in many ways; an expression in which a person can better understand their feelings. During many of the most tumultuous times in my life there was always a poem to be written— one to help me remember the lesson I was meant to learn. Poems became a source of solace, a place to hide. I began journaling at first simply to have an outlet in which to express my innermost emotions but it soon became a valuable resource that helped me to look back and reflect, to really see and understand the events that had taken place in my life. As a matter of fact, I feel a poem coming on now. Will you indulge me to write a few of lines here for you?

Today feels like a new episode in my life.
I awoke feeling stronger yet I do not know why.
How does one know how love affects their lives?
All I feel is love in my heart,
Oh how it makes me sigh.
Today I woke up and knew what I had to do.
I looked out the window and blew a little wish
For you to get stronger because I love you, too.
So many months have come and gone
But for you it's always the same wish
My wish is simple but true, for you to know my love
Will always be for you.

In the midst of the search for finding soul and beauty and creating balance the art of Reiki came into my life. Reiki is based on the concept that our bodies contain healing energy and that we can use this energy to heal ourselves and others. Always being someone who wanted those around me to feel good (and trying to keep peace) this ancient craft seemed to fit my needs perfectly. It felt like a seamless match, not a coincidence at all, and possibly another serendipitous blessing presenting itself. The power of meditation and letting go are significant components in practicing Reiki.

Trusting in all that is right and good is a strong and powerful feeling. The first few times I practiced Reiki the experience was amazing. I realized that I could feel the aura of another person's feelings and help calm them. What was difficult to me was being able to affect a cure for what ailed myself. I felt defeated because I could not reach the level of mastery I strived to achieve.

I felt determined to master this healing art so I meditated more profoundly, opened myself up more to the unknown, the place where Spirit and angels dwell, and asked for divine intervention to help me reach my Reiki healing powers. That's when it happened.

A client that came to my Reiki Master had an unusual pet—a magnificent grey wolf. He had been paired with this woman since he was a pup. She had never brought her wolf with her to a Reiki appointment before but this time she felt the need to be with him. They had just come from the vet's office and, after several treatments, had gotten the devastating news that there was nothing more they could do for him. The wolf was riddled with cancer and was not going to get better. There was no timeline on when he would die, but it would happen. She was going to one day lose her best friend.

I looked at the wolf with such devout and sad eyes and asked if I could sit with him while she had her Reiki session. She told me that he would not normally leave her side when she was around, but he came to me. I thought I felt a kindred kinship with him. I shared with her that my spirit animal is the wolf so if he would allow me to lay hands on him, I might be able to help comfort him. For the next hour, he laid on the rug. I laid my hands on him and prayed with all my soul. I felt my body transcend out and into the stars where I asked for his cancer to be taken away. He had such a beautiful spirit and his master still needed him for her own healing. I had never before felt this connection with the Spirit but I knew I was welcomed that day.

A month had gone by and the woman came back to my Reiki Master. She asked for me and we made arrangements to meet the next day. My prayers were answered when she explained that her wolf, her dear friend, was not going to die anytime soon. She had taken him back to the vet as they were keeping a close eye on his health. To everyone's surprise this wolf had no signs of cancer in his body. It was a miracle that the doctors could not explain. He was completely cured! I hit the floor on my knees and called the wolf to me, thanking God and the angels above for granting our prayers. With monumental gratitude, I again felt validated.

In small ways we can all make changes in our lives. Every day we can speak the language of gratitude even if it's waking in the morning and being grateful for having had a good night's rest. There are people among us who don't have this blessing. As the day unfolds, be grateful for all that you have.

How do you start? One method I suggest is, before you fall asleep at night, write down five things that you are grateful for in a journal. This may help you to see that so much that we have, and can do, goes unnoticed. It only takes a small interruption, an accident or sudden mishap to change everything, and it can happen in a heartbeat. Journaling can be a godsend in many ways. Stories and experiences won't be forgotten once committed to paper.

This brings me back to my dear mother, Margie. Over the years, she has told me many stories about herself and my family. Sometimes I only listened and never wrote them down. Now I struggle to remember all of what she shared with me. Remembering all of the details is an impossible task. When I look at her pictures I find myself wondering who a person was and what year the picture was taken. A simple fix would have been to write dates and names on photos, and I meant to do that, but alas it did not happen. It makes me sad that my mother knows my name sometimes but has no idea who I am, or anyone else for that fact. I am unable to affect a change in her situation or really tell her much of anything new because she has no retention of information.

Gratitude, gratitude, gratitude, I can't remind myself enough! Since there is still no cure in sight for the devastating disease of Alzheimer's, I urge friends and family to look seriously at being more gracious and helpful to others who have less for which to be grateful. If everyone made an effort to uplift one another or lend a hand in any small way, I know this world could be a better place.

This is the biggest challenge I have encountered thus far on my journey. It sometimes makes me feel very lonely though thankfully I am surrounded by caring friends and strangers who offer advice and encouragement. I am grateful for all the caregiving blogs and organizations that have are available to build awareness and help caregivers cope with their issues in this field. At this point in my life, and my children's lives, we are forced to view how truly precious life is and how it can be knocked out of balance without notice. This being said I am grateful that I was able to share this part of my journey.

I hope that our readers will stop and take note of others around them. Do not judge others because you may never know the trials they face or what they are going through. Be kind and caring. We all have to keep moving forward with our lives. We will never know when change will come. We must try to seek the truth of our own existence and strive to make this world a better place. I am at a crossroads in my life but the one thing I know for sure is that I have been blessed with much momentous gratitude and glorious threads of grace.

PAT ROA-PEREZ

A writer and spiritual teacher **Pat Roa-Perez** is on a mission to help women get back to their original self so they can create rich and meaningful lives. Drawing from spiritual lessons that helped her recover from depression and connect with her life purpose, she teaches women how to eliminate the sabotaging noise in their heads that keeps them stuck and unhappy. A firm believer that women are destined to be the next guardians of the world, she encourages, inspires, and challenges women to stop being victimized by their own minds, take back control of their destiny, so they too can help other women do the same. Knowing the struggles of living with depression, Pat is passionate about bringing awareness to the plight of those suffering with mental illness.

ACKNOWLEDGMENT

Thank you, God, for not letting me give up on life and for guiding me out of the darkness of depression. Along the way to recovery, many spiritual teachers helped and inspired me, including Dr. Wayne W. Dyer. My heartfelt thanks to him for teaching me how to challenge the mind and for inspiring me to teach. And in memory of my father who with his last breath encouraged me to fulfill my calling.

DEDICATION

This chapter is dedicated to my beautiful son, Jonathan. May you always dance to the sound of your own music and follow your own path. Thank you for helping me discover my life purpose and teaching me to love again.

Connect with Pat

Email: pat@reinventedwomenonly.com

Website: www.reinventedwomenonly.com

Social Media

www.facebook.com/reinventedwomenonly

www.twitter.com/patroaperez

CHAPTER EIGHTEEN

How God's Perfect Plan Helped Me Overcome Depression and Find My Life Purpose

By Pat Roa-Perez

I count myself among the lucky ones, those who have awakened and are able to witness the incredible power of God. That invisible, organizing power that synchronizes everything we need to live a happy and meaningful life. The power that works on our behalf and leaves nothing for us to do other than trust and follow.
—Pat Roa-Perez

Pretty amazing, aren't they?

Those moments when everything seems to fall into place without much effort on our part, almost as if someone was working on our behalf. The person we've been meaning to call suddenly calls. The answer to a question that has eluded us pops into our head. The problem we've been trying to solve magically resolves itself. And even though we don't understand what's going on, we feel this difference because we know life is not supposed to be this way, this effortless.

We don't want to get used to it. We do not trust it as it goes against the accepted belief that life is supposed to be difficult. So, when we experience how effortless life can be, it feels strange, unfamiliar, and we cannot enjoy it. We can't because we expect, at any moment, our life will go back to what's normal—struggling.

Living Depressed and Without Purpose

I had almost given up.

I had reached the middle of the road of life and still had not found my purpose for being here. Having battled depression most of my life, by now I had lost hope of finding that ever-elusive commodity—purpose.

Depression got in the way.

Depression made it hard to hear my calling, and as I approached the autumn of my life, the desire to fulfill my calling grew stronger, intensifying my fears and sense of urgency, making my depression more severe and debilitating.

Embarking on a Spiritual Journey

God did not give up on me.

He knew when the right season was for me to embark on a journey like none I had ever travelled before. A journey that took me into unchartered waters, of unprecedented spiritual learning and self-discovery, and one that eventually led to recovering from depression and connecting with my life purpose.

It would be years, almost a decade, before I had a full view of God's perfectly choreographed plan that guided me all along and kept me from straying.

It started with the loss of a job.

I lost my job.

This is how my journey began, and I know that because of the way I felt. After fourteen years with the same company, I was let go, and instead of feeling sad, I was happy. Why? It did not make sense. It did not have to. All I knew was that it had to be this way and it was time to move on.

I had wanted to leave for a while but never gained the courage to do it. Now it was real and I knew it was part of something bigger, something that was going to alter the course of my life. As I walked out of the place that had been my professional home for years, I noticed something different. A strange feeling, unfamiliar, and one which I had not felt in a long time—*the absence of fear in my heart.*

Embracing Uncertainty

The absence of fear made this moment unique, made it stand out. After all, I had just left behind a life of stability and stepped into a world of uncertainty, something I had feared since I migrated to the U.S. and was uprooted from everything I knew.

Certainty was something I had craved and strived for ever since and the reason I avoided anything that upset it. Leaving my job would have done that. So I never did…in spite of feeling like I needed to. Here I was, forty-something, with no college degree, raising a three-year-old, and having no fear or worry about the future. Instead, I felt relieved, liberated, and excited about the unknown with a deep conviction that I did not need to know where I was going.

Not this time. Not anymore. For as uncertain as the road ahead was, somehow I knew I would not be travelling it alone.

Rediscovering God

Our lives are shaped by the values and beliefs we have about us, the world, and God or the universe. Often, though, we go through life uncertain as to what they are. As a result, we fail to see whether they can help us or not. God knew most of my values and beliefs were inaccurate and did not serve me well. All through my journey, He made sure to point them out. At the very core of my beliefs was a belief in God, and in the first part of my journey, I was pointed to that in the most unusual manner.

One Sunday morning, while watching television, I came across Joel Osteen, a handsome and charismatic preacher. He spoke of a God unfamiliar to me. A God who wanted us to be happy, prosperous, and did not require pain and sacrifice in exchange. This went against what I believed.

Who is this God he is talking about? I wanted to know so I got his book,

Your Best Life Now, and what I found in its pages forced me to stop and pay attention to my own beliefs. For the first time I saw how flawed they were. For the first time I realized how much they hurt me instead of helped. From that moment on my view of God changed, leading to a strengthening of my connection with Him. Later on I realized the need for this transformed view and stronger connection as they helped me weather the storm on the next part of my journey.

Revealing the Truth About Me

Just as I needed to transform my beliefs about God, I also needed to reexamine what I believed about me, and to do it, God provided me with the perfect stage—starting a business.

After losing my job, the only option I knew was finding a new one. Starting a business never crossed my mind. Yet, that was exactly what I ended up doing. It was not my choice. It was too risky, uncertain, and something I didn't know anything about. Had it been up to me, I would not have chosen this path. *God chose it for me.* He knew it was the best way to unearth the hidden self-beliefs that were at the core of my self-loathing.

Though it did not last, during the four years I was self-employed, I was forced to step out of my comfort zone by doing things I believed I could never do. As a result, I was able to see the negative and limiting self-beliefs I did not know I had and that, once revealed, were transformed into positive and beneficial self-truths.

Out of this experience, a new sense of self emerged—one more confident and able. One that helped me deal with the next part of the journey, which proved to be one of the most difficult and painful times in my life.

Putting It to the Test

By 2009 all hell broke loose. That is how I labeled the events that took place during this part of my journey.

I quit the business I had started. With everything that was going on around me, it was impossible to keep up with it. My mother's health began to deteriorate, followed by my father's colon cancer diagnosis. By this time, they both needed constant care so I began to spend more time with them and less at home with my son, who at that time needed me more than ever before. Because of his condition, Tourette Syndrome, he was struggling in school and I could not be there for him. This made me feel like the worst mother ever.

Everything that could go wrong did. My life seemed out of control. Constantly being pulled in different directions, I had no time to stop and catch my breath. Soon, my health began to deteriorate too, making life even more difficult. Life became unbearable and I could barely function. Everything seemed dark, hopeless; no way out. And yet, in the middle of it all, I remained whole and standing, even if I felt broken and beat down.

Surrendering to What Is

My life situation became too much to handle and my descent into severe depression began. I was so physically and emotionally exhausted that I became ill. For two weeks I could not get out of bed. At first I thought it was the flu, but when I could not shake it, I realized it was something more.

I felt as if part of me was dying. I was in pain and could not move. I couldn't eat and I slept most of the day. Time seemed to stand still, and just when I thought there was nothing left to do, no reason to keep going, an exquisite sense of surrender came over me.

There was no struggle. No resistance. No need to know anything. And deep within—an unbelievable sense of peace. Peace so pure and undiluted, unlike none I had ever experienced before. Peace that felt so real and permanent that a new sense of being emerged.

Everything around me looked and felt different, and yet, everything was the same. The life I had left on hold was still there, waiting for my return.

Awakening

This moment was a turning point. The end of the journey that delivered me from the darkness of depression and into the light of hope. Though it would be a while before I realized what had happened, it was the start of a new journey, one that eventually connected me with my life purpose and led me to fulfill my calling. It is where I learned to live in the present moment.

I count myself among the lucky ones—one who emerged from the dark and was given a second chance at life. I am grateful to God; grateful I can now trust unconditionally the synchronicity of the universe and live a life in which there is nothing to do other than follow.

IN CONCLUSION...

We end as we began—as it is written in the very beginning of this amazing book:

An invisible thread connects those who are destined to meet, regardless of time, place, and circumstance. The thread may stretch or tangle. but it will never break.

> —Ancient Chinese Proverb

This book was literally born from *seemingly* random events that we call synchronicity. Sometimes subtle and sometimes LOUD and CLEAR these stories all showcase the connection to what we call an invisible thread. Different perceptions of what that thread looks like, how it came about and what its purpose is, has filled the pages of this book. It has likely filled the places in your heart that truly knew there was a connection, an energy or an invisible force connecting you to different feelings, people and life experiences. With this connection, whether physical or invisible, and the knowledge of it, I believe you can create anything you desire.

As I have journeyed through my life, and what an incredible journey it has been, I have seen how synchronicity has changed my direction in an instant, how trust has moved me away from harm and how willingness has offered me comfort in painful times. Things I did not know or even understand literally changed my life experience. The connection to Spirit was always guiding me, even when I didn't understand it or was unwilling to listen. It was always there.

As you read the stories of these amazing women, I am sure you saw and felt the consistent theme, message or pattern that I did. Something extraordinary guided them in moments where they lost hope. These messages, as you have read, show up in the perfect time and in the most perfect way. The invisible threads are there for us all in the most amazing ways, if we will simply be open to seeing them. Are you open?

Here are some of the ways the synchronicity of life manifested in some of our authors and how it can too manifest for you, if you are willing to listen:

- As a teacher, offering words of encouragement and support in the exact right time.
- In the form of a vision, offering a glimpse of what could be, if the choice to let go and move forward would be made.
- In a simple message like walk through the door.
- Through the words of a child.
- The messages you receive from the spirit world and your loved ones in spirit.
- Our own acceptance of ourselves and the love we have within
- Releasing the fear and doing it anyway
- Through the death of a loved one
- Through the grace and ease that moves through us when we surrender
- An experience that leaves you with the awareness to choose to take your power back.
- Acknowledgment of your TRUE Intuitive gifts
- An accident—that, in truth, is not really an accident but a life changing Aha.
- Through the words of a song
- Life altering nearly life-ending experiences
- Subtle signs and messages
- A diagnosis of disease or depression

You see, synchronicity is happening all the time; expect it. The invisible thread guides us throughout this journey called life. You may not be consciously aware of it, that is why it is invisible, at least at first. But, as the awareness gathers, as the understanding expands and as the vision is awakened, it is seen. Some see it one way, some see it another, but ultimately, those that are ready will see that connectedness and recognize that we are all One; separated by these physical bodies, but joined through the energy of synchronicity.

I am blessed that our invisible thread, yours and mine, has become visible through the connection within this book. We are all connected now.

All of the beautiful souls in this book, you and I are all a part of each other's experience. However subtle that may be, it is nonetheless true.

Enjoy the connectedness my friend.

Love and Light, Synchronicity and Blessings,

Sunny Dawn Johnston